Norma R. Houston

A Legal Guide to Construction Contracting with North Carolina Local Governments

Fifth Edition 2015

UNC SCHOOL OF GOVERNMENT

The School of Government at the University of North Carolina at Chapel Hill works to improve the lives of North Carolinians by engaging in practical scholarship that helps public officials and citizens understand and improve state and local government. Established in 1931 as the Institute of Government, the School provides educational, advisory, and research services for state and local governments. The School of Government is also home to a nationally ranked graduate program in public administration and specialized centers focused on information technology and environmental finance.

As the largest university-based local government training, advisory, and research organization in the United States, the School of Government offers up to 200 courses, webinars, and specialized conferences for more than 12,000 public officials each year. In addition, faculty members annually publish approximately 50 books, manuals, reports, articles, bulletins, and other print and online content related to state and local government. Each day that the General Assembly is in session, the School produces the *Daily Bulletin Online*, which reports on the day's activities for members of the legislature and others who need to follow the course of legislation.

The Master of Public Administration Program is offered in two formats. The full-time, two-year residential program serves up to 60 students annually. In 2013 the School launched MPA@UNC, an online format designed for working professionals and others seeking flexibility while advancing their careers in public service. The School's MPA program consistently ranks among the best public administration graduate programs in the country, particularly in city management. With courses ranging from public policy analysis to ethics and management, the program educates leaders for local, state, and federal governments and nonprofit organizations.

Operating support for the School of Government's programs and activities comes from many sources, including state appropriations, local government membership dues, private contributions, publication sales, course fees, and service contracts. Visit www.sog.unc.edu or call 919.966.5381 for more information on the School's courses, publications, programs, and services.

Printed in the United States of America

21 20 19 18 17 4 5 6 7 8

ISBN 978-1-56011-760-5

Summary Contents

Contents

Preface

This publication is designed to provide general guidance to North Carolina local governments and private sector contractors, architects, engineers, and others interested in the legal requirements for local government construction and professional design services contracting. Each chapter provides a summary of the legal requirements for various aspects of the construction contracting process, and every topic is accompanied by frequently asked questions and answers. In addition to competitive bidding requirements for public construction and repair projects, this book also discusses exceptions to competitive bidding as well as the legal requirements for contracting with architects, engineers, surveyors, and alternative construction delivery methods under the state's Mini-Brooks Act. It reflects legislative changes through April 2015.

The author wishes to acknowledge the work of retired School of Government faculty member A. Fleming Bell, II, who for many years provided advice to local governments on construction contracting and authored several editions of *Construction Contracts with North Carolina Local Governments.* This volume is the fifth edition of that publication. A special debt of gratitude is owed to Frayda S. Bluestein, David M. Lawrence Distinguished Professor of Public Law and Government, for her invaluable assistance, guidance, and thoughtful comments on the draft of this publication. As with all publications of the School of Government, this book would not have been produced without the hard work, dedication, and unsurpassed expertise of the Publications Division, with special thanks to Katrina Hunt, Kevin Justice, Dan Soileau, Leslie Watkins, and Lisa Wright.

Norma R. Houston
Spring 2015

Chapter 1

Public Contracts Overview

Chapter 1

Public Contracts Overview

Local governments enter into contracts with private entities to procure the goods and services needed to perform governmental functions and serve their constituencies. A number of legal requirements apply to local government contracts that must be complied with in order for the contract to be legally valid. Complying with all applicable competitive bidding requirements, which is the primary focus of this book, involves one important set of statutory requirements. However, additional legal requirements also apply not only to the contracting process, but to the contracts themselves. These additional requirements are discussed in this chapter.

As Figure 1.1 illustrates, the elements of a valid public contract include having

1. an offer that has been accepted and for which consideration has been exchanged;
2. the contract awarded and executed by the proper official or body legally authorized to take these actions;
3. compliance with statutory budget, accounting, and preaudit requirements;
4. a written document;
5. compliance with statutory competitive bidding requirements;
6. compliance with other applicable legal requirements.

A checklist for the elements of a valid public contract is presented in Appendix 1A.

I. What Is "Construction"?

In order to comply with the statutory requirements that apply to local government contracts for construction and repair work, it is important to first understand what the terms *construction* and *repair* mean. Neither term is defined in the bidding statutes applicable to local government construction and repair contracts. When a term is not specifically defined by statute, that term is to be given its plain and ordinary meaning,[1] literally, the meaning given in the dictionary.

1. Lanvale Props., LLC v. Cnty. of Cabarrus, 366 N.C. 142, 154 (2012) ("As we long have held, 'Statutory interpretation properly begins with an examination of the plain words of the statute.'" Three Guys Real Estate v. Harnett Cnty., 345 N.C. 468, 472 (1997) (quoting Correll v. Div. of Soc. Servs., 332 N.C. 141, 144 (1992)). "'If the language of the statute is clear and is not ambiguous, we must conclude that the legislature intended the statute to be implemented according to the plain meaning of its terms.'" *Id.* (quoting Hyler v. GTE Prods. Co., 333 N.C. 258, 262 (1993)). Thus, "'[w]hen the language of a statute is clear and unambiguous, there is no room for judicial construction, and the courts must give it its plain and definite meaning.'" Smith

Figure 1.1. Elements of a Valid Public Contract

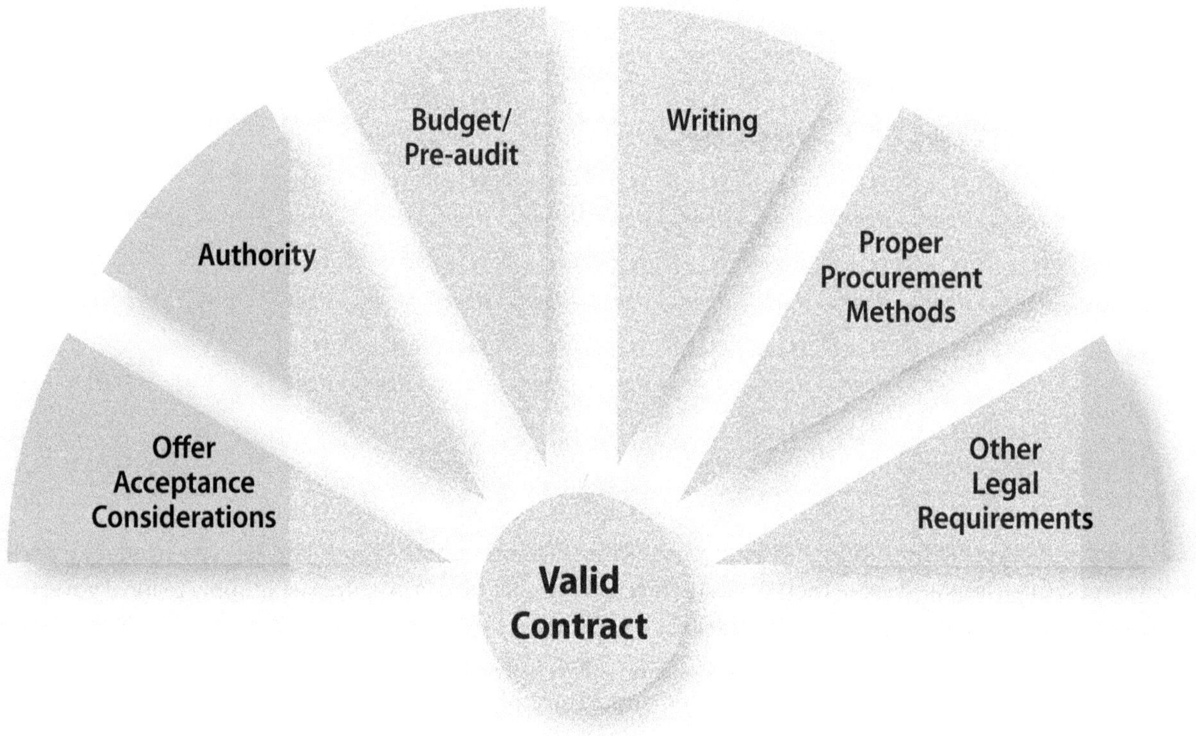

"Construction" is defined in Webster's tenth as "to make or form by combining or arranging parts or elements" (this definition is cross-referenced to "build," defined as "to form by ordering and uniting materials by gradual means into a composite whole"). Repair is defined as "to restore by replacing a part or putting together what is torn or broken" (this definition is cross-referenced to "fix," defined as "to make firm, stable, or stationary; to repair or mend"). The use of "repair" in conjunction with "construction" in the competitive bidding statutes suggests repair of public works (buildings, roads, and utilities), not repair of equipment or other personal property (for example, motor vehicle repair).

While not directly applicable, the regulations adopted by the North Carolina Environmental Management Commission for issuing air quality permits when required under Section 143-215.108 of the North Carolina General Statutes (hereinafter G.S.) are instructive on the definition of construction. In a 2001 Advisory Opinion issued in response to a request for interpretation of the air quality permit regulations, the North Carolina Attorney General noted the definition of construction contained in those regulations. These regulations use the term "construction" as a surrogate for "build" and "erect," as follows: "'Construction' means change in the method of operation or any physical change (including on-site fabrication, erection, installation, replacement, demolition, or modification of a source) that results in a change in emissions or affects the compliance status."[2] Note that, while this regulation includes the term "demolition," a contract for demolition services is not considered a contract for construction or repair work subject to competitive bidding requirements. As discussed above, while construction involves making or building up, demolition involves the opposite type of activities—tearing down. Unless the demolition contract

---

Chapel Baptist Church v. City of Durham, 350 N.C. 805, 811 (1999) (quoting Lemons v. Old Hickory Council, BSA, Inc., 322 N.C. 271, 276 (1988)).

2. N.C. Admin. Code (hereafter N.C.A.C.), title 15A, ch. 2Q § .0103(9); the advisory opinion can be found at 2001 WL 920512 (N.C.A.G. Feb. 8, 2001).

also involves construction-related activities, such as site prep or paving and grading, the contract is treated as a service contract and, as such, is not subject to state competitive bidding requirements.

Another illustrative example is found in G.S. 143-135.3, which defines "construction and repair" for purposes of resolution of claims involving state contracts as "the construction of buildings and appurtenances thereto, including, but not by way of limitation, utilities, plumbing, heating, electrical, air conditioning, elevator, excavation, grading, paving, roofing, masonry work, tile work and painting, and repair work as well as any contract for the construction of airport runways, taxiways and parking aprons, sewer and water mains, power lines, docks, wharves, dams, drainage canals, telephone lines, streets, site preparation, parking areas and other types of construction."

Construction and repair (especially repair) can be distinguished from a service in that a service (also not defined in the statutes) suggests the personal performance of an activity, such as lawn maintenance or solid waste collection, as opposed to delivery of a tangible item, such as a constructed building or a repaved road. Indeed, Webster's defines service as "useful labor that does not produce a tangible commodity." This distinction is important; as discussed in Chapter 2, construction and repair contracts are subject to competitive bidding requirements, whereas service contracts are not. To the extent that it is unclear whether a particular project involves a service as opposed to construction or repair work, the safest course of action is to follow the competitive bidding requirements for a construction or repair contract.

II. Accounting and Budgeting Requirements

Cities, counties, and many other units of local government must follow the requirements of the Local Government Budget and Fiscal Control Act (hereinafter, the Act), G.S. Chapter 159, Article 3, in appropriating and disbursing funds for construction and repair projects and other purposes.[3] In particular, the Act requires both that all construction and other contracts obligating the local government to pay money be covered by an appropriation for the current year's payments in either the budget ordinance or a project ordinance of the local government and that there be sufficient monies remaining in the appropriation to pay any amounts that will come due under the contract in the current fiscal year.[4] All such contracts must also include on their face a certificate signed by the local government's finance officer stating that the contract has been preaudited in the manner required by the Act. Any contract that does not comply with these requirements, including inclusion of a signed preaudit certificate, is void and unenforceable, and any public official or employee who disburses funds on a contract that violates these requirements is liable on his or her official bond for the sums disbursed.[5]

City, county, and local board contracts may continue for more than one fiscal year (which is typical for a major construction project) as long as some related requirements found in G.S. 160A-17 (for cities), 153A-13 (for counties), and 115C-441 (for school boards) are met. Detailed rules for disbursing funds to pay amounts due under construction and other contracts and penalties for violating the appropriation, preaudit, and disbursement provisions are set out in other parts of the Act.[6]

---

3. Public schools and community colleges operate under separate statutes, the School Budget and Fiscal Control Act (G.S. Chapter 115C, Article 31) and the community college budgeting law (G.S. Chapter 115D, Article 4A).

4. G.S. 159-28(a).

5. G.S. 159-28(3); Exec. Med. Transp., Inc. v. Jones Cnty. Dep't of Soc. Servs., 735 S.E.2d 352 (N.C. Ct. App. 2012), *disc. rev. den'd*, 737 S.E.2d 378 (N.C. 2013).

6. For more information on local government finance requirements, including financing capital projects, see *Introduction to Local Government Finance*, 2d ed. (2014), edited by Kara A. Millonzi, and *Financing Capital Projects in North Carolina*, 2d ed. (1994), by David M. Lawrence, both published by and available from the UNC School of Government.

III. E-Verify Contracting Prohibition

All public entities in North Carolina, including cities, counties, school boards, and other units of local government, are prohibited from entering into a contract with a contractor who has not complied with the state's E-Verify hiring requirements (the prohibition extends to the contractor's subcontractors). A contract entered into in violation of this prohibition is presumably void and unenforceable. For cities, counties, school boards, and other units of local government, the prohibition applies only to contracts subject to formal competitive bidding requirements—contracts for the purchase of apparatus, supplies, materials, and equipment estimated to cost $90,000 and above and contracts for construction or repair work estimated to cost $500,000 and above. No other local government contracts are subject to the prohibition.[7]

IV. Prohibited Contract Provisions

State law prohibits certain provisions from being included in contracts because these provisions have been determined by the General Assembly to be against the public policy of this state. If a prohibited provision is included in a contract, that provision is void and unenforceable.

A. Construction Indemnity Agreements

Indemnification is basically protection against liability for damage or loss. A party to a public or private contract for construction or repair work or for design services (architectural or engineering) is prohibited from indemnifying itself against liability from its *own* actions.[8] However, this prohibition does not prevent indemnification of one party from the *other* party's actions. In other words, a contractor can indemnify a local government against liability for damages or losses caused by the contractor's actions, but the contractor cannot indemnify himself or herself against liability arising from the contractor's own actions.

B. Choice of Law

For all public and private contracts involving improvements to real property (including the purchase of materials to be used on a project), any provision that makes the contract subject to the laws of another state is prohibited.[9] Also prohibited is any provision that requires any litigation, arbitration, or other dispute resolution process be set exclusively in another state.

C. Forum Selection

For all public and private contracts entered into in this state, any provision that requires the "prosecution" of any action (i.e., filing a lawsuit) or the arbitration of any dispute that arises from the contract to be instituted or heard in another state is prohibited.[10] However, this prohibition does not prevent the parties from mutually agreeing to select another state as the forum for arbitration or litigation of disputes or claims arising under the contract. In addition, a contract involving interstate commerce will likely be subject to the provisions of the Federal Arbitration Act, which supersedes North Carolina law and may require the forum for arbitration to be located in another state.[11]

---

7. G.S. 153A-499(b) (for counties), G.S. 160A-20.1(b) (for cities), and G.S. 143-129(j) (for all public entities). For more information, see "Understanding North Carolina's E-Verify Contracting Prohibition," www.sog.unc.edu/sites/www.sog.unc.edu/files/E-Verify%20FAQs%20-%20August%202014.pdf.

8. G.S. 22B-1.

9. G.S. 22B-2.

10. G.S. 22B-3.

11. 9 U.S.C. § 1 *et seq.*; Szymczyk v. Signs Now Corp., 168 N.C. App. 182 (2005).

D. Jury Trial Waiver

No public or private contract may contain a provision that forces a party to waive its right to a jury trial.[12] This prohibition does not, however, prevent the parties from agreeing to arbitration or mediation as a means to resolve a dispute prior to initiating litigation.

E. Organized Labor Restrictions

Local governments (and state agencies) are prohibited from requiring, prohibiting, or discriminating against a bidder or contractor for adhering to or not adhering to an agreement with a labor organization for a public construction project. The restriction applies also to the awarding of grant funds and tax incentives.[13] The prohibition applies to all construction and repair contracts subject to informal or formal competitive bidding requirements under Article 8 of Chapter 143; contracts not subject to competitive bidding requirements are not included under the prohibition. The statute also provides a mechanism by which the state or a local government may exempt a particular project from the prohibition if there is a finding (after public notice and public hearing) that the exemption is required to avert a "significant, documentable threat to public health or safety."

F. Employment-Related Restrictions

Cities and counties are prohibited from imposing on contractors, as a condition of bidding, any employment-related restrictions that the city or county cannot impose on all private employers within its jurisdiction.[14] The statute specifically references minimum wage and paid sick leave requirements as examples of prohibited restrictions. Since cities and counties have very little authority to enact ordinances regulating private employment matters, the prohibition virtually eliminates the ability of cities and counties to impose employment-related conditions on bidding. It is important to note that the statute specifically applies only to cities and counties; it *does not* apply to local school boards or other political subdivisions, such as water/sewer authorities. In addition, the statute does not appear to apply to contracts not subject to competitive bidding requirements.

G. Use of Unemployment Relief Labor

The competitive bidding rules of G.S. 143-129 cannot be interpreted to require a public agency to enter into a contract that prevents the use of unemployment relief labor paid for by state or federal appropriations or funds.[15]

V. Use of Licensed Contractors

Most local government construction or repair projects require the use of licensed contractors. G.S. Chapter 87 establishes licensing requirements for general, electrical, plumbing and heating, and refrigeration contractors. These requirements apply to persons or firms that contract to do work for local governments, just as they do to persons or firms that contract to do work for private parties.

While the rules for licensing contractors and the cases construing these rules are generally beyond the scope of this book, the basic statutory requirements governing when licensed contractors must be used are relevant to the legal validity of a local government construction or repair contract.

---

12. G.S. 22B-10.
13. G.S. 143-133.5.
14. G.S. 153A-449(a) (for counties) and G.S. 160A-20.1(a) (for cities).
15. G.S. 143-129(d).

A. Projects to Which Licensure Requirements Apply

G.S. Chapter 87, Article 1, requires that licensed general contractors be used for most construction projects costing $30,000 or more, including projects involving the "construction of any building, highway, public utilities, grading or any improvement or structure."[16] A general contractor is defined as "any person or firm or corporation who for a fixed price, commission, fee, or wage, undertakes to bid upon or to construct or who undertakes to superintend or manage" a construction project.[17] In addition, a construction manager at-risk must be a licensed general contractor (see section VIII.A of Chapter 3 for a discussion of construction management at-risk).[18] To become licensed, a general contractor must meet certain statutory requirements and pass an examination administered by the North Carolina State Licensing Board for General Contractors.[19] Similar licensure requirements apply to trade contractors performing electrical, plumbing, heating and air conditioning, and refrigeration work.[20]

General contractors are licensed to perform construction work in the following five specific categories (referred to as "classifications"):

1. building construction, including private, public, commercial, industrial and residential buildings of all types;
2. residential construction of residences that are required to conform to the residential building code adopted by the North Carolina Building Code Council;
3. highway construction;
4. public utilities construction on the following:
    a. water and sewer mains, water service lines, and house and building sewer lines as defined in the North Carolina State Building Code as well as water storage tanks, lift stations, pumping stations, and appurtenances to water storage tanks, lift stations, and pumping stations;
    b. water and wastewater treatment facilities;
    c. electrical power transmission facilities and primary and secondary distribution facilities ahead of the point of delivery of electric service to the customer;
    d. public communication distribution facilities; and
    e. natural gas and other petroleum products distribution facilities; and
5. specialty construction, including work requiring special skills and involving the use of specialized building trades or crafts.[21]

As noted above, trade contractors who perform electrical, plumbing, or heating and air conditioning work are subject to separate licensure requirements. For some construction projects, these trade contractors are not hired by the local government directly but, instead, serve as subcontractors to the general contractor. In these instances, the general contractor is the only prime contractor on the project (a prime contractor is one who contracts directly with the local government). However, the local government may choose to contract with one or more of these trade contractors directly, making them prime contractors on the project in addition to the general contractor. In such instances, the licensing rules for general contractors do not apply to the trade contractors so long as (1) a licensed general contractor performs all general contractor work; (2) a licensee with the appropriate electrical, plumbing, or heating and air conditioning license performs all work that falls within those classifications; and (3) the total amount of general contracting work does not exceed a percentage of the total bid price established by the State Licensing Board of General Contractors.[22]

---

16. G.S. 87-1(a).
17. *Id.*
18. G.S. 143-128.1.
19. G.S. 87-10.
20. G.S. Chapter 87, Articles 2, 4, and 5.
21. G.S. 87-10(b).
22. G.S. 87-1.1.

B. Application of Licensure Requirements to the Bidding and Contracting Process

A local government cannot consider the bid of or enter into a construction contract with a contractor who is not properly licensed for the type of project called for in the project specifications. To ensure that bidders are aware of the licensure requirements that apply to a project, all architects and engineers who prepare plans and specifications for work to be contracted in North Carolina must, if the project is large enough to require a licensed contractor, inform bidders of the licensure requirements for general contractors in their requests for bids and in their specifications. This notice is given by including in the bid invitations and specifications a copy of G.S. Chapter 87, Article 1, "or such portions thereof as are deemed necessary" to let the invited bidder know that evidence of a license must be shown before the bid is considered.[23]

The contractor's license must be valid at the time he or she *submits a bid* for a construction project. A general contractor who is unlicensed when he or she enters into a contract for which a license is required may not recover for work performed under that contract, even if the contractor subsequently becomes licensed.[24] This prohibition applies also if the contractor's license has expired. However, a general contractor is afforded a sixty-day "grace period" in which to renew an expired license; the license does not become legally invalid until after that sixty-day period.[25] Presumably, a local government may consider the bid of and award a contract to a contractor whose license has expired but is not yet invalid because the sixty-day period has not elapsed. Nonetheless, a local government in this situation should proceed with caution in awarding the contract—a contractor whose license is not renewed would be legally prohibited from performing work under the contract, thus requring the local government to rebid the contract.

C. Penalties

Not only is a local government prohibited from awarding a contract to or considering a bid submitted by a contractor who is not properly licensed; G.S. 87-13 makes it a Class 2 misdemeanor for a contractor who is not properly licensed to contract for or even bid on the construction of any project or work for which a general contractor's license is required. It is a Class 2 misdemeanor also for an architect or engineer to recommend that a local government award a contract to someone not properly licensed, unless the recommendation is made in reliance on erroneous current written information received by the architect or engineer from the appropriate contractor licensing board.

D. Exceptions

Certain construction projects are exempt from the requirement that they be superintended (managed) by a licensed general contractor, including

1. construction or alteration projects personally undertaken on one's own land solely for one's own use, including projects that local governments undertake with their own forces (see section IX.A in Chapter 3 for discussion of the owner-contractor exception);
2. furnishing or erecting industrial equipment, power plan equipment, radial brick chimneys, and monuments;
3. construction of structures used for farming purposes by farmers on their own property.[26]

In addition, a person who erects a North Carolina–labeled, manufactured modular building meeting the requirements of the North Carolina State Building Code does *not* need a general contractor's license if he or she has in force, for each modular building to be erected, a $5,000 surety bond ensuring compliance with the code's regulations governing installation of modular buildings.[27]

---

23. G.S. 87-15.
24. Brady v. Fulghum, 309 N.C. 580 (1983).
25. G.S. 87-10(e).
26. G.S. 87-1(b).
27. G.S. 143-139.1.

Type of Contract	When Bid Documents Are Open to Public Inspection
Construction contracts *below* the informal competitive bidding threshold (those costing less than $30,000)	When received by the local government; if required by the local government to be submitted sealed, when the bid is opened
Construction contracts in the *informal* competitive bidding range ($30,000–$500,000)	When the contract is awarded
Construction contracts in the *formal* competitive bidding range ($500,000 or more)	When bids are opened at the public bid opening (the contents of a sealed bid are not open to public inspection until the bid envelop is unsealed)
Guaranteed Energy Savings contracts	When proposals are opened at the public opening (the contents of a sealed proposal are not open to public inspection until the envelop is unsealed)
Requests for proposals (RFPs) on solid waste management facilities and sludge management facilities	When received by the local government; if required by the local government to be submitted sealed, when the bid is opened
Contracts for architectural, engineering, or surveying services and for alternative construction delivery methods (construction management at risk, design-build, design-build bridging, and public-private partnerships)	When received by the local government; if required to be submitted sealed, when the proposal is opened

VI. Public Records

Virtually all records "made or received in connection with the transaction of public business" are subject to public inspection under North Carolina's public records laws.[28] Unless a clear statutory exception exists, documents that fall within the definition of a "public record" must be made available for public inspection.[29] This broad requirement applies to documents generated by the local government in the course of the bidding and contracting process as well as documents submitted by bidders. The primary consideration is not *if* the document is open to public inspection, but *when.*

A. When Bidders' Documents Are Open to Public Inspection

The point in the contracting process at which documents submitted by bidders are open to public inspection depends on the competitive bidding requirements applicable to the particular contract for which bidders are competing. These competitive bidding requirements are discussed in Chapter 2. For purposes of this section, applications of the public records laws to the various methods discussed in that chapter and elsewhere in this book are summarized in the chart above.[30]

B. Exceptions

A few exceptions to the public records laws apply to contracting for construction and design services by local governments.

28. G.S. 132-1.

29. News & Observer Publ'g Co. v. Poole, 330 N.C. 465, 486 (1992).

30. For a detailed discussion of the application of the public records laws to local government bidding and contracting see Eileen Youens, "When Are Bids and Proposals Subject to Public Inspection?" *Local Government Law Bulletin* No. 119 (Feb. 2009), http://shopping.netsuite.com/s.nl/c.433425/it.I/id.375/.f.

1. *Trade Secrets*

Sometimes bidders will mark their bids as "confidential" or "proprietary." Such designations, in and of themselves, do not exempt the documents from public inspection. However, if specific statutory requirements under the North Carolina Trade Secrets Protection Act are met,[31] the information meeting these requirements in the bid documents must be kept confidential by the local government.

Trade secret information received in any bidding or proposal process is not subject to public inspection as long as the information meets the following requirements:

1. The information is "business or technical information, including but not limited to a formula, pattern, program, device, compilation of information, method, technique, or process that:
   (a) derives independent actual or potential commercial value from not being generally known or readily ascertainable through independent development or reverse engineering by persons who can obtain economic value from its disclosure or use; and
   (b) is the subject of efforts that are reasonable under the circumstances to maintain its secrecy."[32]
2. The information is the property of "an individual, corporation, government, governmental subdivision or agency, business trust, estate, trust, partnership, association, joint venture, or any other legal or commercial entity."[33]
3. The information is disclosed or furnished to the local government in connection with the owner's performance of a public contract; in connection with a bid, application, proposal, or industrial development project; or in compliance with laws, regulations, rules, or ordinances of the United States, the state, or political subdivisions of the state.
4. The information is designated or indicated as "confidential" or a "trade secret" *at the time of its initial disclosure to the local government.*[34]

If a local government receives a public records request for documents that contain trade secret information that meets the criteria outlined above, the local government must redact that information before making the documents available to the person who made the request. Because the Trade Secrets Act gives the owner of a trade secret the right to bring a civil action for misappropriation of the owner's trade secrets (which includes unauthorized disclosure) and the owner of the trade secret may recover actual damages as well as punitive damages for misappropriation, a local government should consult with its attorney before making bid documents available for public inspection if the bidder claims that the documents contain confidential trade secret information.[35]

2. *Sensitive Public Security Information*

G.S. 132-1.7(a) exempts from the definition of a public record the "detailed plans and drawings of public buildings and infrastructure facilities" and "information containing specific details of public security plans and arrangements." Specified plans to prevent or respond to terrorist activity also are protected from disclosure. However, information relating to the "construction, renovation, or repair of public buildings and infrastructure facilities" is not included within this exemption, and, thus, such information is a matter of public record.[36] That this statute exempts "detailed plans and drawings" of public facilities but does not exempt "information relating to . . . construction, renovation, or repair" of those facilities may be confusing. Nonetheless, the phrase "detailed plans and drawings of public buildings and infrastructure facilities" provides a clear exception to the public records laws for these documents. So, for example, while architectural plans or "as-built" drawings would be included under

31. G.S. Chapter 66, Article 24.
32. G.S. 66-152(3).
33. G.S. 66-152(2).
34. G.S. 66-152(2), (3); G.S. 132-1.2; emphasis added.
35. G.S. 66-153, -152(1), -154.
36. G.S. 132-1.7(c).

the exemption, other documents related to the bid process, such as the bids submitted by bidders, would not be covered and thus are open to public inspection. Note that there is no requirement that such information be kept confidential, only that it is not covered by the public records law. As opposed to trade secret information, which must be kept confidential, public security information may be disclosed by a local government if it chooses to do so.

3. *Cost Estimates and Bidders Lists*

Related to the contracting process, though not specifically to bidders' documents, is the ability of local governments to keep confidential both cost estimates on projects and what are referred to as "bidders lists." G.S. 133-33 authorizes local governments to adopt rules under which the following information may be kept confidential:

1. the local government's "cost estimate for any public contracts prior to bidding" and
2. the identity of "contractors who have obtained proposals for bid purposes for a public contract" (i.e., the bidders list).

Note that the project cost estimate may be kept confidential only *prior* to bidding; once the bidding process is complete, this information is no longer confidential.

Cost estimates and bidders lists are not exempt from the public records law by operation of the statute. This information may be kept confidential only if the local government adopts a rule providing for such (typically such a rule takes the form of an ordinance, but the statute does not specifically require that an ordinance be adopted). If the local government adopts such a rule requiring that this information be kept confidential, any officer or employee who improperly discloses this information is subject to disciplinary action.

VII. Conflicts of Interest

Several statutes prohibit conflicts of interest in public construction contracting. Violations of many of these statutes are punishable as criminal offenses. And, in one instance, a violation of the statute renders the contract void. While a detailed discussion of these statutes is beyond the scope of this book, they are worth summarizing here because of their impact on the contracting process and those officers and employees involved in that process.[37]

A. Financial Interest in a Public Contract

G.S. 14-234 prohibits a public official or employee who is involved in making or administering a contract on behalf of the public entity he or she serves from deriving a prohibited direct benefit under that contract. A prohibited direct benefit includes having more than a 10 percent ownership interest in the entity with which the local government contracts, receiving income or commission directly under the contract, or acquiring property under the contract. The prohibition extends to the spouse of the public official or employee but not to any other family member. This statute also prohibits a public official or employee who would derive a prohibited direct benefit under a contract from influencing anyone else in the award of that contract. In addition, a public official or employee may not solicit or receive a gift or favor in exchange for influencing or attempting to influence the award of a contract, regardless of whether the official or employee receives a prohibited direct benefit under the contract. A violation of this statute is punishable as a Class 1 misdemeanor and renders the contract void.

Exempt from prohibitions under G.S. 14-234 are contracts with banks, savings and loan associations, and regulated public utilities; contracts for reimbursement for providing direct assistance under state or federal public assistance programs under certain conditions; for conveying property through condemnation; for employment

37. For more information on the application of conflicts of interest prohibitions to local government officials and employees, see A. Fleming Bell, II, *Ethics, Conflicts, and Offices: A Guide for Local Officials*, 2d ed. (Chapel Hill: UNC School of Government, 2011), and "Ethics and Conflicts of Interest," in *County and Municipal Government in North Carolina*, 2nd ed., edited by Frayda S. Bluestein (Chapel Hill: UNC School of Government, 2015).

of a public officer's spouse (this exception does apply to spouses of public employees); and contracts entered into by public hospitals and public hospital authorities. In addition, certain small contracts are exempt if the contract is with a city having a population under 15,000 based on the most recent federal census or with a county with no incorporated municipality with a population of more than 15,000. Contracts allowed under this exception are subject to strict procedural requirements and only with board members, not employees. For purposes of this book, it is important to note that this exception is not available for contracts subject to competitive bidding requirements.

B. Misuse of Confidential Information

G.S. 14-234.1 makes it a Class 1 misdemeanor for any state or local government officer or employee to use confidential information for personal gain, to acquire a pecuniary benefit in anticipation of his or her own official action, or to help another person acquire a pecuniary benefit from such actions. Confidential information is any non-public information that the officer or employee has learned in the course of performing his or her official duties.

C. Gifts and Favors

G.S. 133-32 prohibits a current contractor, a contractor who has performed under a contract with a public agency within the past year, or a person who anticipates bidding on a contract in the future to give any gift or favor to public officials and employees who have responsibility for preparing, awarding, or overseeing contracts, including inspecting construction projects. The statute does not define gift or favor. A reasonable interpretation is that the prohibition applies to anything of value acquired or received without fair compensation unless it is covered by a statutory exception. These exceptions include advertising items or souvenirs of nominal value, honoraria for participating in meetings, and meals at banquets. The statute also allows public officials and employees to accept customary gifts or favors from friends and relatives as long as the existing relationship, rather than the desire to do business with the unit, is the motivation for the gift. Finally, the statute specifically does not prohibit contractors from making donations to professional organizations to defray meeting expenses or public officials who are members of those organizations from participating in meetings that are supported by such donations and are open to all members (for example, sponsorship of a conference event that is open to all conference attendees). A violation of this statute is punishable as a Class 1 misdemeanor, and both the contractor who gives a prohibited gift and the public official or employee who receives it are subject to this sanction.

D. Project Designers

Architects and engineers performing work on public construction projects are prohibited from specifying any materials, equipment, or other items manufactured, sold, or distributed by a company in which the project designer has a financial interest.[38] Project designers are prohibited also from allowing manufacturers to draw specifications for public construction projects.[39] A violation of these restrictions is punishable as a Class 3 misdemeanor; violators lose their licenses for one year and pay a fine of up to $500.[40]

E. Bid-Rigging and Restraints of Trade

Bid-rigging and other restraints of trade in public contracting in North Carolina are regulated by G.S. Chapter 133, Article 3, commonly known as the "bid-rigging" statutes. G.S. 133-24 and -25 define the crime of bid-rigging and state the penalties for those convicted of it. In sum, these statutes make it a Class H felony "to engage in bid-rigging or other forms of restraint of trade [that are made unlawful by G.S. 75-1 and -2] relating to either a contract or a subcontract with a public agency that involves construction or repair work or the supplying of equipment,

---

38. G.S. 133-1.
39. G.S. 133-2.
40. G.S. 133-4.

materials, goods, or services."[41] (Violations of G.S. 75-1 and -2 are themselves also Class H felonies, independent of the provisions of G.S. 133-24 and -25.)

The penalties for violating these statutes are severe. The court can fine individuals and companies convicted of violations heavily (up to $100,000 for individuals and $1 million for corporations). It also can (1) prevent those convicted from contracting or subcontracting with governmental agencies in North Carolina, (2) order their contractors' licenses suspended, and (3) for individuals, forbid their employment (as officer, director, employee, or agent) by corporations that contract or subcontract with governmental agencies in North Carolina. All three of these penalties can last for up to three years.[42] Willful commission of perjury "in any affidavit taken pursuant to [the bid-rigging and gifts and favors statutes] or rules pursuant thereto" is punishable as a Class I felony.[43]

Article 3 provides local governments (and other governmental agencies) with several additional weapons to combat bid-rigging. First, G.S. 133-27 provides that persons who are charged with restraint of trade in federal court or the courts of any state may be suspended temporarily by the local government from bidding, subcontracting, and being suppliers to the government. A person convicted of such a charge in federal court or another state's courts may be suspended from such activities for up to three years. Relief in civil court is another possibility. Local governments that have entered into contracts in which a restraint of trade was involved may seek civil damages and use a percentage of those damages as a reward to informants.[44] A local government may also require affidavits of noncollusion from prime bidders.[45] Finally, to prevent collusion among bidders, a local government may choose to adopt a policy under which it may keep confidential its cost estimates and the identity of contractors who have obtained information for bid purposes about contracts for which bids are being received (i.e., the bidders list).[46]

F. Building Inspectors

Both city and county building inspectors are prohibited from having a financial interest in or being employed by a business that furnishes labor, materials, or appliances for building construction or repair within the city or county jurisdiction. All employees of city and county inspection departments, including individuals working under contract with those departments, are prohibited from engaging in any work that is inconsistent with their public duties. In addition to these general prohibitions, the statute requires a city or county to find a conflict of interest if the employee (including individuals working under contract with an inspection department) has a financial or business interest in the project being inspected or has a close relationship with or has previously worked within the past two years for the project's owner, developer, contractor, or manager.[47]

G. Public Hospital Officials and Employees

Boards of directors and employees of public hospitals and hospital authorities and their spouses are prohibited from acquiring a direct or indirect interest in any hospital facility, property planned to be included within a hospital facility, or a contract or proposed contract for materials or services provided to a hospital facility. Limited exceptions to this prohibition apply; a contract entered into in violation of these prohibitions is void and unenforceable.[48]

---

41. G.S. 133-24.
42. G.S. 133-25.
43. G.S. 133-31.
44. G.S. 133-28, -29.
45. G.S. 133-30.
46. G.S. 133-33.
47. G.S. 153A-355 (counties) and G.S. 160A-415 (cities).
48. G.S. 131E-14.2 (public hospitals) and G.S. 131E-21 (hospital authorities).

H. Housing Authorities

Commissioners and employees of a housing authority, or of a city or county when acting as a housing authority, are prohibited from having or acquiring any direct or indirect interest in any housing project, property included or planned to be included in any project, or a contract or proposed contract for materials or services to be furnished or used in connection with any housing project.[49]

VIII. Exempted Local Bodies

Public housing authorities, hospital authorities, joint municipal power agencies, and soil and water conservation districts are exempt from all competitive bidding, bonding, and other general contracting requirements, unless the legislature specifically states otherwise.[50] Each of the enabling statutes for these entities contains language similar to the following provision in the housing authority law: "No provision with respect to the acquisition, operation or disposition of property by other public bodies shall be applicable to an authority unless the legislature shall specifically so state."[51] This sentence has been construed by the North Carolina Court of Appeals to exempt housing authorities from all statutory requirements governing public contracting.[52]

While these public entities are exempt from the competitive bidding requirements generally applicable to other units of local government (cities, counties, school boards, etc.), specific requirements for entering into contracts may be required under their respective statutes. In addition, other contracting requirements, such as the prohibitions discussed in section IV of this chapter, still apply.

IX. Projects Involving Private Parties and Nonprofits

A. Construction by Private Parties on Behalf of a Local Government

Competitive bidding procedures must be followed in some situations that, on the surface, might not seem to require it. For example, a local government might agree with the developer of a residential subdivision for the developer to construct water lines for the subdivision, with the stipulation that the line will be dedicated to the city when it is completed. Even though public funds are not being used directly to construct the line, the North Carolina Supreme Court made clear in a 1960 case that if competitive bidding procedures are not followed the contract will be considered void.[53]

There are three specific exceptions to this rule. The first two are applicable to both cities and counties. The last one applies to cities only.

1. A city or county may agree to reimburse private developers and landowners for the design and construction of specified types of municipal infrastructure that are on the city's or county's Capital Improvement Plan and that serve the developer or property owner. (For purposes of this statute, "municipal infrastructure" includes water mains, sanitary sewer lines, lift stations, stormwater lines, streets, curb and gutter, sidewalks, traffic control devices, and other associated facilities.) The developer or landowner must solicit bids in compliance with G.S. Chapter 143, Article 8, when awarding contracts for work that would have required competitive bidding if awarded by the city or county.[54]

---

49. G.S. 157-7.

50. G.S. 157-9 (public housing authorities); 131E-23(d) (hospital authorities); 159B-11(10) (joint municipal power agencies); and 139-8(11) (soils and water conservation districts).

51. G.S. 157-9.

52. Carolinas Chapter NECA, Inc. v. Housing Auth. of the City of Charlotte, 29 N.C. App. 755 (1976).

53. Styers v. City of Gastonia, 252 N.C. 572 (1960).

54. G.S. 153A-451 (counties), G.S. 160A-499 (cities).

2. A city or county may contract with a private party for public enterprise improvements, as defined in G.S. 160A-311 (cities) or G.S. 153A-274 (counties), that are adjacent or ancillary to a private land development. The contract is to allow the city or county to reimburse the private party for costs associated with the design and construction of improvements that are in addition to those required by the city's or county's land development regulations. For example, a developer might agree to design and construct an oversized water line that is intended to meet the city's or county's anticipated needs as well as the requirements of the current private development. Such a contract is not subject to G.S. Chapter 143, Article 8, if
   a. the public cost will not exceed $250,000 and
   b. the city or county also determines that
      (i) the public cost will not exceed the estimated cost of providing the improvements through either eligible force account qualified labor (see section V.C of this chapter) or through a public contract let pursuant to Article 8, or
      (ii) the coordination of separate construction improvements would be impracticable.[55]
3. A city may contract with a private party for public intersection or roadway improvements that are adjacent or ancillary to a private land development. The contract is subject to generally the same limitations as the public enterprise improvement contracts discussed in (2) above.[56]

Another common situation involves the construction of a building by a private developer under an arrangement whereby the building or large portions of it will be leased to a governmental unit. If the building is being constructed to the government's specifications, or would not have been built but for the government's request or needs, the competitive bidding laws almost certainly apply. This is even more likely the case if the government is the only or the major tenant and if the government is to assume ownership of the building at some time in the future.

The inverse of the situation described above occurs when the government rents part or all of a public facility to a private entity who then undertakes repairs and upgrades to the facility, sometimes at the direction of the governmental unit. A similar situation involves that of a private entity leasing real property from a unit of government and constructing a building or other infrastructure on that property. As with the situation described above, competitive bidding requirements most likely apply in cases where improvements to public property and public facilities are made by private tenants at the direction of the governmental unit.

B. Construction by Nonprofit Corporations

Another issue that sometimes arises involves the extent to which private, nonprofit entities that carry out some of the functions of local governments are bound by the laws that apply to governments. For example, under what circumstances must a nonprofit hospital corporation comply with the competitive bidding statutes if it is doing things that a public hospital owned by a county, city, or public hospital authority would do?

The answer to this question under North Carolina law depends on the extent of the connections between the nonprofit corporation and the local government. In a 1981 court of appeals case, *News & Observer Publishing Co. v. Wake County Hospital System*,[57] the court provided perhaps the most detailed elaboration of the factors that can be important in determining whether a particular nonprofit corporation is subject to laws that apply to local governments. In *News & Observer Publishing Co.*, the court was required to interpret the phrase "agency of North Carolina government or its subdivisions," found in the public records law, in order to determine whether a nonprofit hospital corporation was a county agency for purposes of that law. Noting the fact-specific nature of the determination of whether a particular corporate entity should also be considered an agency of local government, the court concluded that "Wake County's supervisory responsibilities and control over the [Wake County

55. G.S. 153A-280 (counties); G.S. 160A-320 (cities).
56. G.S. 160A-309.
57. 55 N.C. App. 1 (1981), *disc. review denied*, 305 N.C. 302, *cert. denied*, 459 U.S. 803 (1982).

Health System were] manifest" and that its ties to the county led "to the inescapable conclusion that the System exercise[d] its 'independent authority' so intertwined with the county that it must be, and is, an 'agency of North Carolina government or its subdivisions;' i.e., Wake County."[58]

In its decision, the court listed the following factors as relevant to its determination. The articles of incorporation provided that (1) on the system's dissolution, it would transfer its assets to the county and (2) that "[the filling of] all vacancies on the [system's] board of directors would be subject to the [county commissioners'] approval." The lease agreement between the county and the system provided (3) that "the [s]ystem occupy premises owned by the county under a lease for $1.00 a year," (4) that "the [county] [c]ommissioners review and approve the [s]ystem's annual budget," (5) that "the county conduct a supervisory audit of the [s]ystem's books," and (6) that "the [s]ystem report its charges and rates to the county." The operating agreements for the hospital system also provided (7) that "the [s]ystem be financed by county bond orders," (8) that "revenue collected pursuant to the bond orders be revenue of the county," and (9) that "the [s]ystem would not change its corporate existence nor amend its articles of incorporation without the county's written consent." In addition, the court of appeals noted that the system was carrying out a public and governmental function of the county,[59] and found significant the fact that the relationship between the nonprofit hospital system and the county was very similar to the relationship that existed between a predecessor hospital authority and the county. In short, said the court of appeals, the relationship between the county and its hospitals had "undergone little more than a change of name through incorporation."[60]

Which of the factors outlined in *Wake County* are most important in determining whether a nonprofit entity is subject to the laws governing local government construction and repair contracts? Unfortunately, there is no exact answer to the question of how many factors are enough. In general, however, as the number of important factors that are present in a given case increases, so does the likelihood that the nonprofit corporation will be considered a governmental agency and subject to the laws that apply to local governments. On the other hand, if few or none of the listed factors are currently present, the fact that the corporation might at some time in the past have qualified as a public agency, or that it continues to perform a function that is of use to the general public or furthers the public good, or that its connection to the governmental unit is purely based on funding (as is typically the case with volunteer fire and rescue departments) are not enough to make it subject to laws that apply to governmental agencies.[61]

---

58. 55 N.C. App. at 11–12.
59. *Id.*
60. *Id.* at 12.
61. Chatfield v. Wilmington Hous. Fin. and Dev., Inc., 166 N.C. App. 703, 709, 710 (2004).

Appendix 1A Public Contracts Checklist

Basic legal requirements for local government contracts:

1. Were all (if any) statutorily required *procurement procedures* followed? (For example, if formal or informal bidding is required, is the awardee the *lowest responsible, responsive bidder*?)
2. Is the contract required to be in *writing*?
   - ✓ All city contracts (G.S. 160A-16)
   - ✓ Conveyance of real property (including easement), mining rights, or leases exceeding three years (G.S. 22-2)
   - ✓ Construction contracts costing $500,000 or more; purchase contracts costing $90,000 or more (G.S. 143-129)
   - ✓ Sale of goods exceeding $500 (G.S. 25-2-201(1))
   - ✓ Other Uniform Commercial Code and common law contract requirements

     NOTE: Putting *all* contracts in writing is highly recommended, *especially* in light of court opinions requiring that a preaudit certificate be affixed to all public contracts expending public funds, thereby resulting in the need for all such contracts to be in writing.

     NOTE: Defects in writing requirements can be cured by board ratification.
3. Did the proper legal authority *award* the contract?
   - ✓ Governing board approval required for formal construction, informal and formal sole-source, and piggyback contracts (G.S. 143-129); small jurisdiction exception to conflict of interest prohibition (G.S. 14-234(d1))
   - ✓ Delegated authority authorized for formal purchase contracts (G.S. 143-129)
   - ✓ Board approval not required for informal construction and informal purchase contracts (G.S. 143-131)
   - ✓ Board approval not required for contracts below informal range
   - ✓ Check local policies for more stringent board-approval requirements
   - ✓ Confirm delegated award authority either explicitly or implicitly (best to have explicit delegation)
4. Did the proper legal authority *execute* the contract?
   - ✓ Confirm execution authority either explicitly or implicitly (best to have explicit authorization, such as by local policy or in job description)
5. If in *electronic form*, is the form valid? If an *electronic signature* is used, is it in proper form?
   - ✓ Most forms of electronic transactions are valid if the parties agree (Uniform Electronic Transactions Act (Article 40, Chapter 66))
   - ✓ Electronic signatures defined and authorized, and procedural requirements for use set out in Article 11A, Chapter 66
6. Are all *terms and conditions* current and in compliance with state law?
   - ✓ *Construction indemnity agreements*—prohibit a party from insulating itself from its own negligence (G.S. 22B-1)
   - ✓ *Real property improvement dispute venue*—prohibits making a contract subject to the laws of another state or setting exclusive venue in other state (G.S. 22B-2)
   - ✓ *Forum selection*—prohibits requiring prosecution of an action or arbitration of a dispute in another state (G.S. 22B-3)
   - ✓ *Jury trial waiver*—prohibits requiring a party to waive its right to a jury trial (does not prohibit mutually agreed to mediation, arbitration, or other alternative dispute resolution processes) (G.S. 22B-10)
   - ✓ *Constitutional limitations on local government*—indemnify obligations of other parties (incurring debt) (N.C. Constitution, Article V, Section 4)

Appendix 1A Public Contracts Checklist (*continued*)

- ✓ *Organized labor restrictions*—prohibit discriminating against a bidder or contractor for adhering or not adhering to an organized labor agreement (G.S. 143-133.5)
- ✓ *Employment-related restrictions*—prohibit cities and counties from imposing employment-related restrictions, such as minimum wage or paid sick leave, on bidders and contractors if the city or county does not have the legal authority to impose the restriction on all private employers within its jurisdiction (G.S. 153A-449(a) for counties; G.S. 160A-20.1(a) for cities)
- ✓ *E-Verify*—contractors and subcontractors are to comply with the state's E-Verify hiring requirement (G.S. 153A-449(b) for counties; G.S. 160A-20.1(b) for cities; G.S. 143-129(j) for other units of local government)

7. Does the contract adequately describe or incorporate by reference the information that relates to the *scope of work* or *other details specific to the basis for the contract*?
8. Does the contract include a *preaudit certificate*? (G.S. 159-28)
   - ✓ Preaudit certification required for all public contracts obligating public funds to ensure that sufficient funds are available and unencumbered (G.S. 159-28(a))
   - ✓ Some question about preaudit certificate requirement if fiscal obligation is in future year (Meyers v. Town of Plymouth, 135 N.C. App. 707 (1999)); safest course is to *always* include preaudit certificate (violation can result in personal liability for employee or officer disbursing funds)
   - ✓ Preaudit certificate signed by finance officer or deputy finance officer must be affixed to all contracts, resulting in the need for all contracts to be in writing (Exec. Med. Transp., Inc. v. Jones Cnty Dep't of Soc. Servs., 735 S.E.2d 352 (N.C. Ct. App. Nov. 6, 2012)).
9. Does the contract comply with applicable *local policies*, *grant rules* (if grant funds are used), and *federal regulations* (if federal funds are used)?
10. Do any *conflicts of interest* exist that would render the contract void? (G.S. 14-234). If the *small jurisdiction exception* applies, have all required procedures for contract approval been followed? (G.S. 14-234(d1)).

Chapter 2

Competitive Bidding Requirements for Construction and Repair Projects

Chapter 2

Competitive Bidding Requirements for Construction and Repair Projects

I. Summary of Competitive Bidding Requirements

Public entities, including local governments, must comply with all the statutory procurement requirements that apply to a particular contract to avoid the contract being rendered void and unenforceable.[1] In fact, North Carolina law prohibits dividing a contract into separate parts to evade competitive bidding requirements.[2] Local governments may not assume responsibility or guarantee payments for materials or labor for contracts involving construction or repair projects unless all applicable competitive bidding requirements are followed.[3]

A. Basic Procurement Method Analysis: Contract Type Plus Cost Determines Procurement Method

In order to determine which procurement method is required for a specific contract, it is first necessary to identify the type of contract and that contract's estimated cost.

1. *Type of Contract*

For purposes of state competitive bidding requirements applicable to local governments, all contracts into which they enter fall into four categories:

1. *purchase*—purchases of supplies, materials, apparatus, and equipment;
2. *construction or repair*—construction of horizontal or vertical structures or infrastructure or the repair of such structures or infrastructure;

1. Hawkins v. Town of Dallas, 229 N.C. 561, 564 (1948) (citing Abbott Realty Co. v. City of Charlotte, 198 N.C. 564 (1930); *see also* Jenkins v. City of Henderson, 214 N.C. 244, 249 (1938); Raynor v. Comm'rs of Town of Louisburg, 220 N.C. 348 (1941)).

2. Section 143-133 of the North Carolina General Statutes (hereinafter G.S.).

3. G.S. 143-129(b); *Hawkins*, 229 N.C. 561; Nello L. Teer Co. v. N.C. State Hwy. Comm'n, 265 N.C. 1 (1965).

3. *Mini-Brooks Act services*—surveying, architectural, engineering, construction management-at-risk, design-build, design-build bridging, and public-private partnership;
4. *everything else*—general service contracts, leases that do not include an option to purchase, and real property purchases.

2. Cost (Bid Thresholds)

The cost of purchase and construction or repair contracts determines which bidding method must be used to enter into that contract according to the following thresholds:

1. $30,000—informal bid threshold for purchase and construction or repair contracts;
2. $90,000—formal bid threshold for purchase contracts;
3. $500,000—formal bid threshold for construction or repair contracts.

3. Procurement Methods

After the type of contract and its cost are identified, the method of procurement required (or not required, as the case may be) can be determined. There are four categories of procurement methods.

1. *Informal bidding* applies to purchase and construction or repair contracts in the informal bidding range.
2. *Formal bidding* applies to purchase and construction or repair contracts in the formal bidding range.
3. *Qualifications-based selection (QBS)* is required for all Mini-Brooks Act services, unless the unit of local government exempts itself in writing.
4. *Request for proposals (RFP)* is optional for all service contracts other than Mini-Brooks Act services.

The chart presented in Figure 2.1 combines the type of contract, bid thresholds, and procurement methods under North Carolina law for local governments.

B. Local Policies

It is important to note that local governments may adopt local procurement policies under which lower bid thresholds might be established. For example, while state law sets the informal bidding threshold at $30,000,[4] a local government may choose to set a lower informal bidding threshold, such as $5,000. So long as local procurement policies are not in conflict with state law, local governments should adhere to their own procurement policies, especially when those policies set more stringent procurement requirements than those set by state law.

C. Application of Bid Threshold to Contract Cost

The formal bid threshold ($500,000) applies to the estimated cost of the construction or repair contract. On the other hand, the informal bid threshold ($30,000) applies to the actual cost of the contract. In both instances, if a construction or repair project involves multiple contracts, the bid threshold applies to the amount of each contract to be awarded, not the total project cost.

For example, if a local government upgrades its water and sewer system in multiple phases for funding purposes and awards contracts for each phase separately, bid thresholds will apply to the contract for each phase, not the entire project. Thus, if the estimated cost of the first phase is $750,000, formal bidding requirements apply. However, if the estimated cost of the second phase is $450,000, informal bidding requirements may be used.

What if the good faith estimate of the project is under $500,000 but one or more of the bids exceeds $500,000? Because local governments cannot award a construction or repair contract in the formal bidding range unless it has complied with the formal bidding requirements, the local government could award a contract only if the winning bid is less than $500,000. Otherwise, the local government must rebid the project following the formal bidding requirements.

---

4. G.S. 143-131.

Figure 2.1 Procurement Methods

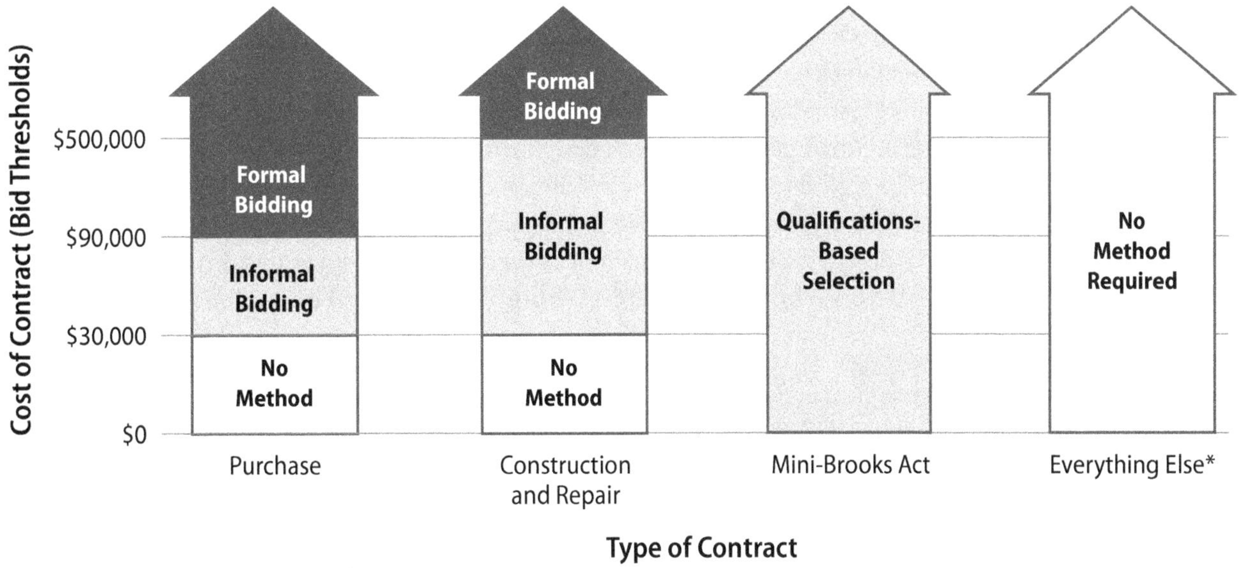

*Use of RFP optional, but not required.

II. Formal Bidding Procedures

The formal bidding procedures prescribed in Article 8, Chapter 143, of the North Carolina General Statutes (hereinafter G.S.) must be followed whenever a North Carolina local government undertakes construction or repair work with an estimated expenditure of public funds of $500,000 or more. This includes projects involving construction or repair of buildings as well as other types of construction projects, such as street paving, communications towers, and water and sewer infrastructure.

The legal requirements outlined in the following sections apply to all construction and repair contracts, including those involving construction or repair of a building, in the formal bidding range. The following sections are organized in a manner that generally follows the construction contracting process; included within each section are frequently asked questions and answers associated with a particular topic.

A. Developing Plans and Specifications

Before a construction or repair project can be advertised, plans and specifications for the required work must be prepared. Architects and engineers preparing plans and specifications on behalf of the local government must include in the specifications information about any licensure requirements applicable to the project.[5] If the project involves the erection, construction, alteration, or repair *of a building*, then additional statutory procedures also apply (see Chapter 3 for a discussion of these additional requirements).

2.1. How do we hire an architect or engineer to draw the specifications?

If a local government hires an architect or engineer to draw up plans and specifications for a construction or repair project, it must follow the qualifications-based selection process required under Article 3D of Chapter 143 (commonly referred to as the Mini-Brooks Act), unless the unit has exempted itself in writing from these requirements (see Chapter 7 for a full discussion of the Mini-Brooks Act).

5. G.S. 87-15. See Section V of Chapter 1 for a discussion of licensure requirements.

2.2. What are the limitations on including brand name products in plans and designs?

To ensure and encourage free and open competition on public construction contracts, state law places limits on specifying particular brand names of materials included in plans and specifications for construction or repair projects. Under G.S. 133-3, architects, engineers, designers, and draftsmen who provide design services or write specifications, directly or indirectly, for materials to be used in any city, county, or state construction or repair work must specify in their plans the required performance and design characteristics of those materials. If these characteristics are impossible or impractical to specify, then brand name products may be listed in the specifications so long as at least three items of equal or equivalent design are listed, thereby establishing an acceptable range for such items. If performance and design characteristics cannot be specified, and if fewer than three items of similar or equivalent design are available, then as many alternatives as are available must be specified.

When brand name products are included in specifications, those specifications must clearly state all of the following:

1. the cited examples are used only to denote the quality standard of product desired and do not restrict bidders to a specific brand, make, manufacturer, or name;
2. the examples are used only to show bidders the general style, type, character, and quality of product desired; and
3. equivalent products will be acceptable.

Maximum interchangeability and compatibility of specified items is required, and the brand of product used must not limit competitive bidding on future works.

If a local government or design professional prefers a particular brand of material, the specifications may, in limited circumstances, list it as an "alternate" (alternative) to the base bid. Specifications containing a preferred brand alternate must identify the performance standards that support the preference (in other words, what characteristics of that brand item make it preferred over other brands of the same or similar items), and those standards must be approved in advance by the governing board in an open meeting. The local government may grant this approval only if both of the following conditions are met:

1. the preferred alternate will provide cost savings, maintain or improve the functioning of a process or system affected by the preferred item or items, or both; and
2. a justification identifying these criteria is made available in writing to the public.

Contractors who propose substitutions of materials, items, or equipment of equal or equivalent design must submit them for approval by the architect or engineer. The architect or engineer must make a decision before the bids are opened.

2.3. Are there special requirements for projects involving a building?

Yes. If a construction or repair project involves a building, additional requirements apply, including review by the state insurance commissioner for fire safety of buildings that are 20,000 square feet or larger[6] and the requirement that plans and specifications must be drawn by a licensed architect or engineer.[7] These and other special conditions for building construction or repair projects are discussed in Chapter 3.

2.4. What if convict labor is used on the project? Must bidders be notified?

Potential bidders must be told in advance if a local government plans to use "convict or other labor" to perform part of the work on a proposed construction project. G.S. 143-130 specifies that whenever convict or other labor may be furnished by the state or local government to a contractor who is performing construction work or installing apparatus, supplies, materials, or equipment, the project specifications are to "carry full information as to what

---

6. G.S. 58-31-40.
7. G.S. 133-1.1.

wages shall be paid for such labor or the amount of allowance for same." This requirement helps bidders on such projects prepare proposals that accurately estimate the labor costs involved.

B. Advertising/Soliciting Bids

The unit of government initiates the bidding process by formally advertising a solicitation for bids on the project.[8]

2.5. How are formal bids advertised?

The advertisement must be placed in a newspaper of general circulation in the county, city, town, or other political subdivision involved. Bids also may be solicited by "electronic means," or both methods may be used. A decision to advertise solely by electronic means must be approved at a regular meeting of the unit's governing board and may be approved for particular contracts or generally for all formally bid contracts. While "electronic means" is not defined in the statute, it is commonly understood to mean advertisement on appropriate Internet sites that would reach prospective bidders.

2.6. What must the advertisement include?

The advertisement must state

1. the time and place where plans and specifications of proposed work may be obtained by potential bidders,
2. the time and place for opening the proposals, and
3. that the local board or governing body reserves the right to reject any or all proposals received.

Because the advertisement must state the time and location of the bid opening, this information effectively operates as the deadline for receiving bids. The location of the bid opening should be clearly identified by address and room number. The advertisement should also include the address to which bids may be mailed or delivered. Finally, it is helpful to indicate which clock will be used to determine the time at which the bids will be opened in order to avoid confusion caused by differing clocks or other time pieces.

Copies of the plans and specifications should be placed in a location within the unit of government that is readily accessible to potential bidders, and this location should be clearly stated in the advertisement. Some local governments provide plans and specifications electronically on their websites or through their project designer; if so, the website or other information about electronic access should be included in the advertisement. Local governments may provide a copy of plans and specifications to potential bidders and may charge bidders for the cost of reproduction.

2.7. How long must the advertisement run?

The advertisement must be run at least once prior to the bid opening. At least seven calendar days must elapse *between* the date the advertisement is run and the date the bids are opened. For example, as demonstrated by Figure 2.2, if an advertisement runs on January 1, the bid opening cannot be scheduled any sooner than January 9. Note that the time frame is specific to *calendar* and not *business* days. Because the statute does not authorize a default to the next business day if the bid opening date falls on a weekend or legal holiday, care should be exercised in calculating the number of calendar days between the date of advertisement and the bid opening to avoid inadvertently advertising a bid opening on a weekend or legal holiday.[9]

8. G.S. 143-129(b). See G.S. 1-597 for the definition of a "newspaper of general circulation."

9. For more information on calculating advertisement time frames see Eileen R. Youens, *Counting the Days*, Coates' Canons: N.C. Local Gov't L. Blog (Feb. 9, 2011), http://canons.sog.unc.edu/?p=3932.

Figure 2.2 Date Bids Are Opened Following Advertisement Run on January 1

January 2014

SUN	MON	TUE	WED	THU	FRI	SAT
			1	2	3	4
5	6	7	8	9	10	11
12	13	14	15	16	17	18
19	20	21	22	23	24	25
26	27	28	29	30	31	

C. Receiving Bids: Bid Deadline, Form of Bids, and Bid Deposits

After the bid solicitation has been advertised, the local government receives bids. The formal bidding statute (G.S. 143-129) requires that bids for construction or repair projects be received timely (i.e., by the bid deadline), be sealed and in paper form,[10] and be accompanied by a bid deposit when submitted.

1. Bid Deadline

As stated above, the advertised date and time of the public bid opening operates as the deadline for receiving bids. All bids in the formal bidding range must be received by the unit of government by the date and time stated in the bid advertisement and at the identified location or address.

2.8. What if a bid is received after the bid deadline?

A bid that is received after the date and time stated in the advertisement must be rejected and cannot be considered.

2.9. What if the bid is delivered late by the United States Postal Service, FedEx, or other method of delivery through no fault of the bidder?

The result is the same as if the bidder delivered the bid late. Bidders assume responsibility for delivery, regardless of the agent. Thus, if a bidder uses FedEx and FedEx does not deliver the bid by the bid deadline, the bid must be rejected as untimely.

2.10. What if the bid was received on time but was misplaced by an employee or agent of the unit of government?

If the bid was received by the unit of government prior to the bid deadline and then subsequently misplaced or not delivered to the appropriate department by an employee or agent of the unit, it cannot be rejected as being untimely.[11] The unit must open and consider the bid, even if the public bid opening date has passed. In such a situation, the unit should immediately notify not only the bidder whose bid was misplaced and subsequently opened, but also all other bidders who submitted bids.

---

10. While electronic bidding is authorized for purchase contracts in the formal bidding range, this authorization has not been extended to formal construction or repair bids. G.S. 143-129.9(a)(2).

11. *See* Watterson Constr. Co. v. U.S., 2011 U.S. Ct. Fed. Cl. No. 10-587C (Mar. 29, 2011). The U.S. General Accounting Office has determined that, for federal bids, the government has received a bid at the time the bidder relinquishes control.

2.11. Should late bids be opened?

No. Opening a late bid serves no purpose because the bid cannot be considered by the local government and must be rejected as being nonresponsive. Keeping in mind that the bid documents become open to public inspection once they are unsealed, the late bidder may prefer to have the bid returned unopened.

2. *Bids Must Be Sealed*

All bids in the formal bidding range must be submitted sealed.[12] A bid that is received unsealed does not comply with this statutory requirement and must be rejected; the unit of government may not consider it.

2.12. What does it mean for a bid to be sealed?

The bidding statutes do not define "sealed," but in the bidding context the term is commonly understood to mean closed, fastened, or secured to prevent tampering.[13] Thus bid documents submitted by bidders should be enclosed in an envelope or package that is sealed shut by some form of adhesive (envelope glue, tape, etc.). An envelope or package that is closed with a tuck-in flap, paper clip, binder clip, rubber band or in some other nonadhesive manner should not be considered sealed for purposes of competitive bidding requirements.

2.13. What if the bid is not sealed when it is submitted?

An unsealed bid does not meet the statutory requirement that bids be submitted sealed and therefore must be rejected by the unit of government. In fact, to avoid allegations of tampering or disclosing bid contents, local government personnel should not accept an unsealed bid.[14] If the bid is received unsealed, the local government could notify the bidder and allow that bidder to retrieve the bid and resubmit it sealed so long as the bidder does so by the bid deadline.

2.14. What if a local government employee opens a sealed bid prior to the bid opening?

A sealed bid cannot be knowingly opened or its contents disclosed prior to the public bid opening without the bidder's permission; doing so constitutes a Class 1 misdemeanor.[15] If a bid is accidentally opened prior to the public bid opening, the unit of government should immediately notify the bidder who submitted that bid. To ensure that sealed envelopes or packages containing bid proposals are not accidentally opened by employees not involved in the bid process, it is helpful to instruct bidders to clearly indicate on the outside of the bid envelop or package that a bid proposal is contained inside.

3. *Bids Must Be Received in Paper Form*

Formal construction or repair bids may be received in paper form only. Unlike formal purchase bids, state law does not authorize receipt of formal construction or repair bids through an electronic bidding system.[16] In addition, no formal bids may be received by fax, email, or phone.

4. *Bid Deposit*

At the time it is submitted to the unit of local government, a formal construction or repair bid must be accompanied by a bid deposit of at least five percent of the amount of the bid proposal. The deposit is retained by the unit of local government. The purpose of the bid deposit is not to guarantee performance under the contract; instead, the deposit acts as the bidder's guarantee that he or she will honor the bid amount and comply with the statutory requirements for contract execution.

---

12. G.S. 143-129(b).
13. Merriam-Webster's Collegiate Dictionary (10th ed. 2002).
14. Some local government purchasing officers take a roll of tape to the public bid opening in case a bidder arrives at the opening with an unsealed bid and have the bidder seal the bid before accepting it.
15. G.S. 143-129(b).
16. G.S. 143-129.9(a)(2).

2.15. What form of security may a bid deposit take?

The bid deposit may take only one of the following four forms:

1. cash,
2. a cashier's check,
3. a certified check on a bank or trust company insured by the Federal Deposit Insurance Corporation, or
4. a bid bond executed by a corporate surety licensed to do so under North Carolina law.

If the bidder chooses to submit a bid bond in lieu of a deposit, neither the local government nor anyone acting on its behalf may require the bidder to use any particular surety, agent, producer, or broker as long as the North Carolina licensure requirement is met.[17] However, the governing board may reject the bonds of any surety company against which there is pending any unsettled claim or complaint more than 180 days old that was made by the local government and arose out of any contract involving the expenditure of local funds.[18]

2.16. What if a bid is not accompanied by a bid deposit?

The formal bidding statute specifically states that bids not accompanied by a satisfactory deposit may not be "considered or accepted" by the unit of local government. That the bid cannot be considered if it is not accompanied by a sufficient deposit impacts how such a bid is counted for purposes of determining whether at least three bids have been received in order to open bids (see D.2 of this section for further discussion of the three-bid minimum rule).

2.17. Can a bidder submit a bid deposit after his or her bid has been submitted or after the bid opening?

G.S. 143-129(b) clearly requires the bid deposit to accompany the bid "at the time of its filing," meaning when the bid is submitted by the bidder to the local government. If the bidder realizes that he or she forgot to include a bid deposit *prior* to the bid opening, the bidder may withdraw the bid and resubmit it with a satisfactory bid deposit (the unit should not accept the bid deposit separate from the bid package itself). If, however, the bidder realizes the error *after* the bid opening, he or she is not permitted to correct the mistake by submitting a bid deposit at that time. In this instance, the bid must be rejected as being nonresponsive, and the unit cannot count the bid toward the three-bid minimum required for opening bids in the formal bidding range (see D.2 of this section for further discussion of the three-bid minimum rule).

2.18. What if the bid deposit is for an amount less than five percent of the bid price?

Because state law requires the bid deposit to be in an amount of at least five percent of the bid amount, the result is the same as if the bid was not accompanied by a bid deposit at all (see questions 2.16 and 2.17 above). The bid cannot be considered or accepted by the unit of local government.

If the bid deposit is made in the form of a bond, local governments should carefully review the language of the bond submitted by each bidder. Some standard forms contain language that is not consistent with North Carolina law. For example, a bond form that limits the surety's liability to the difference between the forfeiting bidder's contract and the contract awarded is not consistent with state bid bond requirements because that difference may not equal five percent of the forfeiting bidder's bid price. Nor can the surety's payment obligation be conditioned on the local government awarding the contract to another bidder. North Carolina law requires the forfeiture of the bid bond, and the resulting obligation of the surety, to be immediate, unconditional, and in an amount of at least five percent of the bidder's bid price. A bond that does not meet these statutory requirements is not sufficient, and the bidder's bid must be rejected as nonresponsive.

2.19. May the local government require a bid deposit greater than five percent?

Yes. Because the formal bidding statute requires that the bid deposit be in an amount equal to *not less than* five percent, local governments are not prohibited from requiring a deposit of a greater amount. However, local governments should be mindful of the increase in bidding cost incurred by bidders that may limit the ability of

17. G.S. 58-31-66.
18. G.S. 143-129(c).

some bidders to submit a bid and, in all instances, would likely be passed on to the local government in the form of higher bid amounts.

2.20. May the local government accept a bid bond by fax?

The competitive bidding statutes do not specifically require that a bid bond be submitted in original form, and there is no case law in this state on this point. Given the legal recognition of electronic documents in many instances, including electronic contracts and signatures,[19] a court would likely hold that a faxed bid bond is valid assuming it meets all the statutory requirements. To ensure fairness to all bidders, a local government should state in its specifications whether it will (or will not, as the case may be) accept faxed bid bonds.

2.21. Must bid deposits be returned to bidders, and, if so, when?

The unit of government may not retain bid deposits indefinitely or permanently. Each bidder's deposit must be returned after the contract is awarded, including the deposit of the bidder to whom the contract is awarded. Since the purpose of the bid deposit is to guarantee the bid amount, not contract performance, there is no legal justification for retaining the deposit of the successful bidder except in two instances, which are discussed in the following question.

2.22. When may a local government keep a bid deposit?

The unit of government may retain the bid deposit of a bidder to whom a contract is awarded if the bidder fails to execute the contract within ten days after the award or if the bidder fails to provide satisfactory performance and payment bonds.[20] In each instance, the unit of government retains that bid deposit as damages or compensation for the bidder's breach of its statutory obligation to execute the contract or to provide the performance and payment bonds. (See H.2 of this section for a discussion of performance and payment bonds.)

D. Opening Bids: Public Bid Opening and Three-Bid Minimum Rule

1. Bid Opening

Formal bids are opened in public at the time and place specified in the bid advertisement.[21] The bid opening is conducted by one or more officials or employees of the unit of government or an agent acting on the unit's behalf, such as an architect or engineer hired for the project (in the case of a construction management at-risk project, the construction manager conducts the bid opening; see section VIII.A of Chapter 3 for further discussion of construction management at-risk). Once bids are opened, bid documents become open to public inspection (see section VI of Chapter 1 for a discussion of the application of North Carolina's public records law to the bid process). After the bid opening, the local government begins the process of evaluating the proposals to ensure compliance with all statutory requirements and determining the successful bidder.[22]

2.23. Who may attend a bid opening?

Since formal bids must be opened in public, anyone can attend, including bidders, interested citizens, and even the media.

2.24. What if the location of the bid opening must be changed? Do we have to cancel the opening?

The bidding statutes do not address this specific situation. However, since the statute requires the date, time, *and location* to be included in the published notice, a change in location could render the advertisement legally invalid. If there is sufficient time to publicly advertise the change in location, the unit should do so, even if it means delaying the bid opening. If not, and if the local government is willing to assume the risk that the advertisement may be legally invalid, it should make every effort to notify the public and bidders of the new location, such as posting

---

19. G.S. 66-317.
20. G.S. 143-129(b).
21. *Id.*
22. Remember that the local government may reject all bids and thus is not required to award the contract.

a sign on the door of the original location indicating where the new location will be, emailing or calling potential bidders (this can be more easily accomplished if the unit maintains a bidders list), and posting a notice on its website. Because the date and time of the bid opening operates as the deadline for receiving bids, units should take into consideration the impact that a change in location will have on determining whether a bid is timely submitted. If there is evidence that a bid was timely submitted at the original location, the bid should not be rejected simply because it was not received at the new location.

2.25. What if a bidder arrives a few minutes late to a bid opening with a bid proposal? Can we still accept it?

No. As discussed above in C.1, a bid that is received by the unit after the advertised time of the bid opening is untimely and must be rejected. This is true even if the bid arrives only a few minutes late, unless the delay was caused by some action by the unit of government, such as an unclear description of the location of the bid opening. For this reason, it is important to clearly state the exact location of the opening in the bid advertisement.

2. Three-Bid Minimum Rule

G.S. 143-132(a) provides that no board or governing body of North Carolina or its subdivisions may award a construction or repair contract to which the formal bidding procedure applies unless it has received at least three competitive bids from "reputable and qualified contractors regularly engaged in their respective lines of endeavor." (This rule does not prevent negotiating a contract with the lowest responsible bidder when at least three bids are received but all of them are too high. See E.1 of this section for further discussion of when negotiations with bidders are permitted.) If three such bids are not received, the local government may not open any bids and must re-advertise the project.

2.26. Can a defective bid be counted toward the three-bid minimum?

Generally, yes. Defective bids probably may still be counted for purposes of the three-bid rule in most instances. Although there are no North Carolina court decisions on this point, it seems reasonable to include in the count serious attempts to bid, even though they may ultimately be deemed nonresponsive due to a failure to meet the local government's specifications. However, bids that are defective because they are untimely or do not include a bid deposit may not be counted.

2.27. Can a late bid be counted?

No. A late bid that was not received by the bid deadline may not be considered by the local government, so it cannot count toward the three-bid minimum.

2.28. Can a bid that is missing a bid deposit be counted?

No. G.S. 143-129(b) specifically states that a bid cannot be "accepted or *considered*" unless it is accompanied by a sufficient bid deposit. Because the statute prohibits consideration of a bid that is not accompanied by a bid deposit, such a bid cannot count toward the three-bid minimum. This result is true also if the bid deposit is insufficient, such as for being in an amount less than five percent of the bid amount or in a form not authorized by statute (see C.4 of this section for further discussion of bid deposits).

Because a bid that does not include a satisfactory bid deposit cannot be counted toward the three-bid minimum, some local governments require bidders to submit the bid deposit in a separate envelope within their bid packages so that the unit may first determine if all bids meet the bid deposit requirement before unsealing the bid documents themselves. This system preserves the confidentiality of bidders' proposals in the event the unit must re-advertise the project because it has not received at least three bids.

For example, if only three bids are received at a bid opening, under the "separate envelope system" the local government can first determine if all three bids meet the bid deposit requirement before opening the bid packages. If one or more of the bids does not include a bid deposit (or the bid deposit is insufficient), the unit may then stop the bid opening without disclosing the bid documents themselves and return the unsealed bid packets to the bidders.

2.29. Can a bid that is missing HUB documentation be counted?

Yes. Although a bid that is subject to statutory requirements mandating good faith efforts by bidders to solicit participation by historically underutilized businesses (HUBs) must be rejected as nonresponsive if the bidder fails to list HUB subcontractors on the bid and include an affidavit attesting to the bidder's good faith efforts, the bid still may be counted toward the three-bid minimum (see Chapter 4 for a discussion of HUB requirements).

2.30. Can a bid for which we have received a bid-withdrawal request be counted?

Yes. The bid-withdrawal statute, G.S. 143-129.1, specifically provides that a bid for which a withdrawal request has been made "shall be deemed to have been received" for purposes of the three-bid minimum requirement.

2.31. Can a "no-bid" bid be counted?

No. The statute requires that bids to be counted toward the three-bid minimum be "competitive bids." A statement by a bidder that he or she is not submitting a bid (a "no-bid" bid) is not a competitive bid and therefore does not count toward the three-bid minimum.

2.32. If we prequalified contractors, can a bid submitted by a bidder who was not prequalified be counted?

Yes. Although such a bid must be rejected as being nonresponsive,[23] it still may be counted toward the three-bid minimum (see section IV of this chapter for a discussion of prequalification).

2.33. What if we do not receive three bids?

If fewer than three bids are received, the local government cannot consider the bids that were received. If it still wishes to proceed with the project, the unit must re-advertise the solicitation of bids following the same statutory procedures that applied to the initial advertisement (see section II.B of this chapter for further discussion of formal advertising requirements). After re-advertisement, the governing body is free to award the contract to the lowest responsive, responsible bidder, even if fewer than three bids are received. In other words, the local government is not required to re-advertise repeatedly until at least three bids are received; only one re-advertisement is required.

If re-advertisement is required, bids received in response to the first advertisement should be returned to the bidders unopened. Bid bonds and bid deposits of the first-round bidders are, of course, returned.

2.34. Are there special rules for counting bids under the dual-bidding system?

Yes. When bidding a construction or repair contract under the dual-bidding system (which involves simultaneously bidding a building construction project under both the single-prime method and the separate-prime (or multi-prime) method), special rules apply.[24] The dual-bidding method and the special rules that apply in counting bids under this method are discussed in section VII.C of Chapter 3.

2.35. How are bids counted under the separate-prime (multi-prime) bidding system?

Under the separate-prime (multi-prime) bidding system, the unit solicits separate bids for each of the primary subdivisions or branches of work to be performed—heating, ventilation, and air conditioning (HVAC), plumbing, electrical, and general. Because the unit will award separate contracts for each category, the three-bid minimum rule will apply to each category for which the estimated cost of the contract is $500,000 or greater (see section VII.A of Chapter 3 for further discussion of separate-prime bidding).

E. Evaluating Bids: Negotiations with Bidders, Bid Errors, and Bid Withdrawal

Once bids are opened, the local government must evaluate them to determine if the bids conform to the project specifications and meet all applicable statutory requirements. Bids that do not conform to statutory requirements or do not substantially conform to the project specifications must be rejected as being nonresponsive (see F of this section for further discussion of the lowest responsive, responsible bidder standard of award). The unit of

23. G.S. 143-135.8(d).
24. G.S. 143-132(b).

government also has the right to reject all bids for any reason other than for the purpose of evading competitive bidding requirements.[25]

1. Negotiations with Bidders

During the bid evaluation process, local government personnel may not negotiate price or other aspects of proposals with bidders. While this does not prevent obtaining clarification on nonmaterial items relating to the bid (such as confirming the bidder's mailing address or phone number), local governments must be careful to not pose any questions or seek clarification on any matter that would enable the bidder to change the bid or correct an error or omission or that might create the impression that negotiations are taking place. Unless the item in question is entirely nonmaterial to the bid proposal, local governments should refrain from discussing or seeking clarification on the bid.

2.36. Can we contact a bidder to clarify ambiguities or omissions in a bid?

Local governments are not prohibited from contacting bidders after the bid opening to resolve questions about ambiguities or omissions in a bid. However, such inquiries should be kept to a minimum. Since bidders have the opportunity to see their competitors' bids after the bids have been opened, the local government should avoid engaging in discussions that allow a bidder to improve his or her position or to correct an error or omission, especially one that might otherwise be a basis for rejecting the bid.

2.37. Can we negotiate with bidders if all bids exceed funds available?

There is one instance in which negotiations with bidders is permissible. If all bids for a construction project exceed the funds available to the local government for the project, the unit may negotiate with the lowest responsive, responsible bidder, "making reasonable changes in the plans and specifications as may be necessary to bring the contract price within the funds available."[26] If the bidder agrees to the changes, the unit may then award the contract to the bidder at the reduced price and incorporating the agreed-upon changes. If multiple contracts are involved in the project, the agency may negotiate with all of the lowest responsible bidders on each contract.

2.38. What are considered "reasonable changes"?

While the term "reasonable changes" is not defined in the statute, it should not be interpreted too broadly. If, for example, a complete redesign of a project is needed or if the necessary design changes might result in a change in the order of bidders, the unit should reevaluate the project, potentially making design adjustments or increasing the funding amount (or both), and rebid the project.

2.39. Can the contract be awarded at a lower price and then increased to the original bid amount through a change order if more funds become available?

No. This is not a legally valid use of the change order exception to competitive bidding requirements (see section I of Chapter 5 for a discussion of the change order exception).

2.40. If negotiations with the lowest bidder fail, can we negotiate with the next lowest bidder?

No. The local government has *no authority* to negotiate with the second lowest bidder, even if the lowest bidder will not agree to the changes needed. If negotiations with the lowest bidder fail, or if the local governing board chooses not to negotiate, then the unit may make changes in the plans and specifications to bring the project cost within the amount of funds available and re-advertise for bids. This procedure may be repeated if necessary to secure an acceptable contract within funding limitations. If the re-advertised project differs in any significant way from the original proposal, the project is, in essence, a new project, so the local government should treat the re-advertisement as a first advertisement for purposes of the three-bid minimum rule (see D.2 of this section for further discussion of the three-bid minimum rule).

---

25. G.S. 143-129(b).

26. *Id.*

2. *Correcting Bid Errors*

Bidders are bound by their bid proposals, and just as local governments cannot negotiate with bidders after bids have been opened, bidders cannot correct errors or omissions in their bids after the bid opening. Allowing a bidder to correct errors or make changes to a bid after bids have been opened creates an opportunity for that bidder to change the bid price after having seen those of his or her competitors, thus giving that bidder an unfair competitive advantage. If the error is minor and the bid otherwise substantially conforms to the unit's bid specifications, the local government may waive the error. However, if the error represents a major deviation from the bid specifications, the error cannot be waived and the bid must be rejected.

2.41. If a bidder has inadvertently omitted part of the bid package, may the bidder submit the missing information after bids have been opened?

No. The bid must be evaluated in the form submitted by the bidder. Allowing a bidder to add additional or missing information to the bid package after the bid opening may give that bidder an unfair competitive advantage over other bidders, which is contrary to the lowest responsive, responsible bidder standard of award (see F of this section for further discussion of the standard of award).

2.42. May a bidder correct minor clerical errors after bids have been opened?

No. While the unit may waive the error if the bid is otherwise compliant with all statutory requirements and substantially conforms to the unit's bid specifications, bidders may not correct even minor clerical errors in their bids after bids have been opened.

3. *Bid Withdrawal*

Generally, a bidder may not withdraw a bid after the bid opening, even if the bid contains an error or omission; doing so results in forfeiture of the bid deposit. However, G.S. 143-129.1 authorizes bid withdrawal after the bid opening in certain limited circumstances. If bids have not been opened, a bidder may withdraw a bid at any time without penalty. In this instance, the local government must return the bidder's bid deposit.

A bid withdrawal request is most likely to come from a low bidder whose bid contains a significant calculation error that adversely impacts the bid price, thereby raising questions as to whether that bidder can fully perform the work for the quoted price. Other bidders have no incentive to make a withdrawal request because they are not likely to be awarded the contract (not being the lowest bidder) and will have their bid deposits returned once the contract is awarded.

2.43. When may a bidder withdraw a bid without penalty?

A bidder may withdraw a bid after the bid opening without forfeiting the bid deposit only if all of the following conditions specified in G.S. 143-129.1 are met:

1. The bid was submitted in good faith.
2. The price bid was based on a mistake that constituted a substantial error.
3. Credible evidence is submitted showing that the error was
   (a) clerical in nature, as opposed to an error in judgment, and
   (b) to the result of an unintentional and substantial mathematical error or an unintentional omission of a substantial quantity of work, labor, apparatus, supplies, materials, equipment, or services made directly in the compilation of the bid.
4. The error can be demonstrated by objective evidence obtained from an inspection of the original work papers or from documents or materials used in preparing the bid.
5. The request to withdraw is made
   (a) in writing to the local government that invited the proposals and
   (b) prior to the award of the contract but not later than seventy-two hours after the opening of bids.

2.44. Can we extend the deadline for submitting a bid withdrawal request?

The statute authorizes local governments to specify a withdrawal period that is longer (but not shorter) than seventy-two hours. If the local government chooses to do this, it must specify the period in its bid specifications or instructions to bidders prior to the bid opening; the seventy-two-hour time limit may not be extended after bids have been opened.

For example, a local government might decide to allow for a period that is longer than seventy-two hours, if the seventy-two-hour period would end on a holiday or a weekend. If the local government wanted to allow this limited extension, it could include language in its specifications requiring written notice of a request to withdraw a bid to be submitted by a date certain that did not fall on a weekend or holiday (such as the date of the next business day). In this instance, the unit should specify not only the date, but also the time by which a withdrawal must be received (such as "by 5:00 p.m.").

2.45. What is the procedure for considering a bid-withdrawal request?

Once the local government receives a bid-withdrawal request, it must promptly hold a hearing on the request. The bid withdrawal statute does not specify who is to conduct the hearing. The governing board may conduct the hearing itself, or this function may be performed by an employee of the unit. Regardless of who conducts the hearing, the local government should involve its attorney in the withdrawal proceedings.

The local government must give the bidder who requests withdrawal reasonable notice of the time and place of the hearing. The bidder is allowed to appear and present any additional facts and arguments in support of the request. Should the bidder wish only to submit evidence and not appear personally or through an attorney, it seems reasonable that this also should be allowed.

The board or employee conducting a bid-withdrawal hearing should be careful to follow fair and unbiased procedures. Reliable evidence should be presented and made a part of the record of the decision.

Within five days after the hearing, the local government must issue a written ruling allowing or denying the request. If it finds that the bid was based on a mistake of the type authorized under the bid-withdrawal statute, the request must be granted. Otherwise, the request must be denied. The unit's findings as well as its ruling should be in writing and, if the board conducts the hearing, recorded in the board's minutes. The public agency and its officials, employees, representatives, and agents are protected by G.S. 143-129.1 from incurring any liability in granting a withdrawal request except when fraud or collusion is involved.

2.46. What happens to the bidder's bid deposit?

If a bidder's withdrawal request is denied, the bid deposit must be forfeited. According to G.S. 143-129.1, denial has the same effect as if the bidder had received an award but declined to accept it or as if the bidder had refused to enter into the contract. If the bid-withdrawal request is granted, the unit must return the deposit to the bidder.

2.47. May the bidder appeal a denial of the bid-withdrawal request?

Yes. The bidder who requests withdrawal may appeal a denial by filing a civil action in any North Carolina court of competent jurisdiction within twenty days after receiving the local government's ruling. The entire action is to be tried anew by the judge without a jury.[27] If the denial is upheld, the requesting bidder's bid deposit must be forfeited.

2.48. Can we consider other bids and award a contract if we receive a bid-withdrawal request?

Yes. Although the unit cannot consider the bid for which a withdrawal request has been submitted, it can consider the other bids and award a contract. In fact, the bid-withdrawal statute *requires* the local government to consider and act on the remaining bids as if the bid in question had not been received. It may, however, count the bid as being received for purposes of satisfying the three-bid minimum requirement (see D.2 of this section for further discussion of the three-bid minimum rule).

---

27. G.S. 143-129.1 also permits the matter to be referred to a referee "in the instances and in the manner" provided in Rule 53, as amended, of the North Carolina Rules of Civil Procedure, found in G.S. 1A-1.

2.49. Can a bidder who has withdrawn a bid still perform work on the project?

Only with the written approval of the local government. The bid-withdrawal statute prohibits a bidder whose withdrawal request has been granted from supplying material or labor to, or performing any subcontract or work agreement for, any person awarded a contract or subcontract for the performance of the contract for which the withdrawn bid was submitted, without the local government's prior written approval. Violation of this requirement is a Class 1 misdemeanor.

There are no specific standards set out in the statute for granting approval to a withdrawing bidder to work on the project. However, the public agency would do well to keep in mind overall fairness to other bidders in deciding whether or not to allow it.

2.50. If we re-advertise the project, can a withdrawn bidder rebid on that project?

No. The bid-withdrawal statute specifically prohibits a bidder who has made a bid-withdrawal request from rebidding on that project if the local government re-advertises it.

2.51. What if the withdrawal of a bid would result in the award of a contract on another bid that involves the withdrawing bidder?

A bid may not be withdrawn if withdrawal results "in the award of the contract on another bid of the same bidder, his partner, or to a corporation or business venture owned by or in which he has an interest." This prohibition prevents a bidder who has requested a withdrawal of a bid from still being eligible for the award of a contract under another bid submitted on that same project. For example, suppose the low bidder requests withdrawal and this same bidder has an ownership interest in the second lowest bidder. The statute prohibits the low bidder from withdrawing his bid. However, the local government may still reject the low bidder if it determines the bid is not responsive or the bidder is not a responsible bidder.

F. Determining the Successful Bidder—The Lowest Responsive, Responsible Bidder Standard of Award

For projects in both the informal and formal bidding ranges, if the local government chooses to award a contract it must do so to the *lowest responsive, responsible bidder* while taking into consideration quality, performance, and time specified in proposals for performance of the contract.[28] This legal standard upon which contracts are awarded is referred to as the "standard of award."

The board need not always award a contract to the bidder who is willing to do the work for the lowest cost; rather, the statute permits—indeed, requires—the board to consider a number of factors relating to quality, performance, and time in making its decision as it determines what is in the best interest of the local government. Thus the standard of award allows the governing board a certain amount of leeway in deciding which among several similar proposals to select.

1. Lowest Cost

Determining which bid proposed the lowest price for the project is usually a straightforward determination. The local government compares the total proposed price submitted by each bidder and identifies which price is the lowest. This process can become more complicated, though, if the local government requests pricing for add-on or alternate components of the project, such as options for flooring materials or exterior finishing. In such an instance, the local government should clearly state in its instructions to bidders how it will calculate the lowest cost if it decides to award the contract based on alternates.

---

28. G.S. 143-129(b), G.S. 143-131(a). Recall that local governments may reject all bids for any reason determined to be in the best interest of the local government other than for the purpose of evading competitive bidding requirements.

2.52. What if a bidder leaves a specific line item on the bid form blank?

Depending on the circumstances, the unit may consider the bidder's price for that item to be "zero." If the omission substantially affects the bid price, the bid must be rejected as being nonresponsive. Under certain circumstances, the bidder may be permitted to withdraw the bid (see E.3 above for further discussion of when bids may be withdrawn without penalty). What is not permitted under any circumstance is allowing the bidder to fill in the missing information or adjust the bid price.

2.53. What happens if there is a discrepancy between the bidder's unit price and the total price for that line item (the extension)?

Some projects call for both a unit price of certain materials (such as gravel on a road-paving project) and a total price based on the bidder's estimate of the quantity needed for the project multiplied by the unit price. The total price is typically referred to as an extension. On occasion, a bidder will miscalculate the extension, resulting in a discrepancy between the unit price multiplied by the quantity and the total price. The general rule of practice that addresses this discrepancy is that unit price controls. If the local government wishes to use this rule in the event of a discrepancy between unit price and extension, it should state this in its bid specifications. What is not permitted is allowing the bidder to recalculate the erroneous extension or adjust the bid price.

2. Responsive Bid

For a bid to be responsive it must meet all applicable legal requirements and substantially conform to the local government's bid specifications.[29] A bid that does not meet a legal requirement must be rejected as being nonresponsive. Similarly, a bid that contains a "material variance" from the bid specifications (meaning it does not substantially conform to the bid specifications) also must be rejected.[30] However, because the standard of award recognizes that there may be variations among proposals and that a minor deviation does not disqualify a bidder, a local government may waive minor deviations from the bid specifications. In fact, many local governments include in their instructions to bidders standard language that the unit "reserves the right to waive minor irregularities."

2.54. What legal defects require a bid to be rejected as nonresponsive?

Because local governments do not have the legal authority to waive statutory requirements, a bid that does not comply with a statutory requirement must be rejected. For construction and repair contracts in the formal bidding range, these statutory requirements include the following:

1. The bid must be submitted by the bid deadline.
2. The bid must be in paper form.
3. The bid must be submitted sealed.
4. The bid must include, at the time it is submitted, a bid deposit or bond in a form required by statute of at least five percent of the bid amount.
5. If the project is subject to HUB requirements, the bid must identify the minority businesses to be used on the project and include an affidavit attesting to the bidder's good faith efforts to solicit minority contractors (see Chapter 4 for further discussion of HUB requirements).
6. The bidder must be properly licensed (see section V of Chapter 1 for further discussion of licensure requirements).

2.55. What is a "material variance" from the bid specifications?

The North Carolina Court of Appeals defines a "material variance" as one that gives a bidder "an advantage or benefit not enjoyed by other bidders."[31] In other words, if the variance gives one bidder an unfair competitive

---

29. Prof'l Food Servs. Mgmt. v. N.C. Dep't of Admin., 109 N.C. App. 265 (1993).

30. *Id.* at 269.

31. *Id.* For an excellent discussion of the responsiveness standard see Frayda S. Bluestein, *Understanding the Responsiveness Requirement in Competitive Bidding*, LOCAL GOV'T L. BULL. No. 102 (May 2002), www.sog.unc.edu/pubs/

advantage over other bidders, the variance is material. For example, if the bid specifications require a certain type of high-quality flooring material and a bidder's bid proposes a lower quality flooring material that is substantially less expensive, this would be a material variance. Accepting this bid would be unfair to other bidders whose bid amounts were greater due to their inclusion of the higher quality (and more expensive) flooring material called for in the unit's specifications. In addition to variances that lower the bid price, variances that save a bidder time, that allow a bidder to not honor his or her bid, or that constitute collusion should be considered material.

Whether a variance is material must be determined on a case-by-case basis. The local government may deem a variance to be material based on how important that feature is to the project. It must consider also whether the feature that varies from the specifications represents a cost to other bidders who complied with the specifications or whether the variation is one that the average bidder would have considered to be within the scope of the specifications as written.

2.56. What if the bidder fails to sign the bid form or related bid documents?

The main issue regarding signatures on bids or bid documents is whether, taken as whole, the bid would constitute a binding offer by the bidder as a matter of contract law. The question of whether a bidder would be bound by a particular bid that lacks signatures depends entirely upon the documents involved. If the bidder signs the bid form but fails to sign accompanying documents, this is a variance that can be waived because the bidder's signature on the bid form indicates his or her intent to be bound by the bid. Similarly, if the bidder fails to sign the bid form but includes in the bid package a signed letter indicating his or her authority to submit the bid and intent to be bound by it, this too is a variance that can be waived. However, if the bidder fails to sign any bid documents and does not include any documentation verifying his or her intent to be bound by the bid, this variance is material because the omission gives that bidder the ability to not honor the bid. It should be noted that documents for which state law requires a signature, such as a bid bond or a HUB good faith efforts affidavit, must be signed, and the lack of signature on such documents cannot be waived by the local government. If such documents are required by law, as is the case with a bid bond and HUB affidavits, the lack of signature renders the bid nonresponsive.

2.57. What if the bidder fails to use the proper bid form?

A reliable rule of interpretation in cases involving a bidder's failure to use the proper form is that if the bid amount and other terms of the offer are clear from the face of the bid documents as submitted, the failure to use the form is a waivable defect. Where all of the information necessary to understand and evaluate the bid is contained on the document, failure to complete the proper form is purely a technicality and does not provide any benefit or advantage to the bidder. It is important to note, however, that if failure to use the proper form results in a need to clarify the bid, this may give the bidder an opportunity to improve his or her position after bids are opened. Such clarification should be avoided, and in these circumstances the bid must be rejected.

2.58. Can we reject a bid that has only a minor or technical variance?

Probably not. The North Carolina Court of Appeals has defined a responsive bid as one that "conforms substantially with the terms of the request for bids."[32] In this case, the court overturned the North Carolina Department of Administration's rejection of the low bid. The bidder had provided the requested price information on a food services bid in a format that did not precisely match the bid form. The court held that the state's rejection of the bid as nonresponsive was not supported by the evidence, since the bid was clearly understandable on its face. This ruling suggests that, where a bid is clearly understandable based on the information provided in the bid documents, a minor or technical variance *should* be waived because the bid *substantially* conforms with the unit's bid specifications. In other words, a bid that does not match the bid specs precisely in every respect should nonetheless be considered responsive unless the variance is material.

---

electronicversions/pdfs/lglb102.pdf.

32. *Id.*

3. *Responsible Bidder*

Assuming the lowest cost bid is also responsive, the local government then determines whether the bidder is a responsible bidder. Under this aspect of the standard of award the local government evaluates the bidder's ability to fully perform under the contract as opposed to the sufficiency of the bid proposal itself. North Carolina courts have interpreted "responsible" to imply the bidder's "skill, judgment and integrity necessary to the faithful performance of the contract, as well as sufficient financial resources and ability."[33] If a local government determines that the lowest responsive bid was submitted by a bidder who is not a responsible bidder, the unit may reject the bid.

2.59. What factors may we consider in determining whether a bidder is a "responsible" bidder?

Factors that the local government may consider in determining whether a bidder is responsible are those that relate directly to the bidder's "skill, judgment, financial resources, and integrity." Information related to these factors include financial information, references from previous projects, listing of personnel to be used on the project and their qualifications, safety records, information on performance on past projects, and claims/litigation history.

It is important that the local government limit its determination of responsibility to factors that relate to the bidder's ability to successfully perform under the contract being bid. Information about the bidder that goes beyond this scope is not relevant under the standard of award. For example, a bidder's history of construction-related litigation and claims is relevant, but a bidder's prior parking tickets is not.

2.60. What documentation is required if we determine a bidder is not responsible?

The statutes do not require any specific documentation. However, if the local government rejects the lowest responsive bid because it has determined that the bidder is not a responsible bidder, the local government should document the basis of its decision in case the bidder challenges the local government's decision. An easy way to obtain this documentation is to require bidders to submit such information as financial statements, references, safety records, personnel qualifications, etc., with their bids. If the local government checks a bidder's references, it should document the conversation or request feedback from the reference in writing. In addition, failure to provide such information in the bid specifications when requested to do so may be grounds for rejecting the bid as nonresponsive.

2.61. What if we've worked with a bidder before and the project did not go well? Can we determine that he is not aresponsible bidder on this basis?

A local government's experience with a contractor can be the best evidence of whether the contractor is or is not a responsible bidder. The local government may have examples of unjustified delays, excessive or unjustifiable change orders, failure to pay subcontractors on a timely basis without good reason, or poor workmanship. If so, these factors may be considered by the local government in determining whether this contractor is a responsible bidder. Also, as discussed above, while documentation is not statutorily required, the local government nonetheless should document examples of poor performance on past projects in the event that the bidder challenges its decision.

Local governments should avoid determining a bidder is not responsible simply because an employee or department head does not like or get along with that bidder. The responsible bidder standard is not a popularity contest; local governments should have clear examples of prior poor performance, documented if possible, when it determines that a bidder is not a responsible bidder based on prior experiences with that bidder.

G. Contract Award

Once the local government has determined the lowest responsive, responsible bidder, assuming it still wishes to move forward with the project, it awards the contract to the successful bidder.

---

33. Kinsey Contracting Co. v. City of Fayetteville, 106 N.C. App. 383, 385, *disc. review denied*, 332 N.C. 345 (1992).

2.62. Who has the authority to award the contract?

Contracts in the formal bidding range must be awarded by the local government's governing board.[34] While the governing board may delegate this authority to an employee for formal purchase contracts, it cannot do so for formal construction or repair contracts. Consequently, all contracts for construction or repair work in the formal bidding range must be awarded by the governing board without exception. The mayor or board chair cannot award the contract on behalf of the governing board; action must be taken by the board itself.

2.63. What if the contract is not awarded by the governing board? Can this error be fixed?

Yes. If the contract is inadvertently awarded by an employee or officer of the local government, or perhaps by its architect or engineer, that error can be corrected if the governing board subsequently gives its approval to the contract award. However, the contract will not be considered to have been awarded until the governing board has taken action.

2.64. Since the governing board must approve the award of a formal contract, must it also reject formal bids?

The statute does not address who has the authority to reject formal bids. Since the governing board is the only entity with legal authority to award construction or repair contracts in the formal bidding range, it stands to reason that it is also the board who must reject bids for such contracts.[35]

2.65. How long does the governing board have to award the contract after bids have been opened?

The competitive bidding statutes do not specify a time frame within which a governing board must make a contract award decision. Many legitimate reasons may delay a board's decision, such as the length of time necessary to fully evaluate bids on a complex project or the need to consult with the architect or engineer on particular aspects of the bids. However, local governments should not unnecessarily delay the award decision. Many local governments include in their bid specifications time frames requiring bidders to honor their bids for a certain period of time after the bid opening, such as sixty or ninety days. They also may include a statement that the contract award and notice to proceed will be issued within a certain period of time. If the local government violates its own self-imposed deadlines, bidders may argue that they are no longer legally bound by their bids.

Even absent such deadlines, if the delay is excessive, a bidder might argue that requiring him or her to proceed under the original bid is unfair in that prices and assumptions that were relied upon when the bid was submitted have expired or are so out-of-date that the original bid process is invalid or that the bidder would be forced to perform the project at an unreasonable price, which would constitute a financial burden.

2.66. How do we document the board's award of the contract?

All actions taken by a governing board must be recorded in the board minutes. Thus in the case of contract awards, the clerk to the board will record in the minutes the board's vote to award the contract (or its vote to not award the contract, as the case may be). While not legally required, it is a good practice also to include a summary (not the details) of the other bids along with documentation verifying compliance with other statutory requirements, such as proper advertisement and receipt of an adequate number of bids. An affidavit of advertisement from the newspaper in which the notice was advertised will satisfy the former, and a copy of the bid tabulation form will satisfy the latter.

---

34. G.S. 143-129(a).

35. For further discussion of rejecting bids see Norma Houston, *Rejecting Bids—Who Can and When Can They?* Coates' Canons: N.C. Local Gov't L. Blog (Apr. 13, 2011), http://canons.sog.unc.edu/?p=4359.

H. Contract Execution: Who May Execute and Performance and Payment Bonds

After the governing board has awarded the contract, the written contract document itself is executed (signed) and the successful bidder provides performance and payment bonds.[36] While the formal bidding statute does not specify in which order these two actions must occur, it is highly recommended that the local government obtain the contractor's performance and payment bonds before it executes the contract.

1. Contract Execution

2.67. Who has the authority to execute the contract?

The competitive bidding statutes do not specify who is authorized to execute (sign) a contract on behalf of the local government. Because execution of a contract is a formality that is used to prove assent (or agreement) to be bound by the contract, the contract should be executed by an officer or employee who has the legal authority to give such assent on behalf of the local government, such as the mayor, board chair, or manager.

2.68. What is the difference between awarding a contract and executing a contract?

As discussed above, contract execution is a formality proving assent to be bound by the contract. Contract award, on the other hand, represents the actual decision to be bound by the contract, and it must be made by an individual who or entity that has the legal authority to bind the unit of government. For construction and repair contracts this can be done only by the governing board itself. That an individual officer or employee has the authority to execute a contract does not necessarily mean that he or she also has the authority to award (or approve) a contract.

2.69. How much time does the bidder have to execute the contract?

The formal bidding statute requires the successful bidder to execute the contract within ten days after the contract is awarded.[37] If the bidder fails to do so, the bid bond is forfeited. However, if the local government delays transmitting the contract document to the bidder, the bidder should not be penalized, and adequate time should be given to allow the bidder an opportunity to review and execute the contract.

2.70. How much time does the local government have to execute the contract?

While the successful bidder must execute the contract within ten days after contract award, the same requirement does not apply to the local government. As discussed in G of this section, the local government should avoid undue delays in executing the contract, as the same issues that apply to delay of the contract award decision may also arise if the local government unnecessarily delays contract execution.

2.71. Must the contract be in writing?

Yes. Contracts subject to formal competitive bidding requirements must be in writing.[38] In addition, any changes or alterations to the contract also must be in writing and agreed to by the contractor and the local government's governing board.

2. Performance and Payment Bonds

Under North Carolina law, performance and payment bonds must be furnished to the local government by *each* contractor with a contract costing over $50,000 on construction or repair projects where the total of all contracts for the project exceeds $300,000.[39] Each bond must be for 100 percent of the contract amount and must be executed by a surety licensed in North Carolina. If the contractor does not provide performance and payment bonds, he

---

36. G.S. 143-129(c).
37. G.S. 143-129(b).
38. G.S. 143-129(c).
39. G.S. 143-129(c); G.S. 44A-26(a). Note that the $300,000 amount is less than the $500,000 threshold for projects in the formal bidding range.

Figure 2.3 Requirements for Performance and Payment Bonds under Separate-Prime Contracting

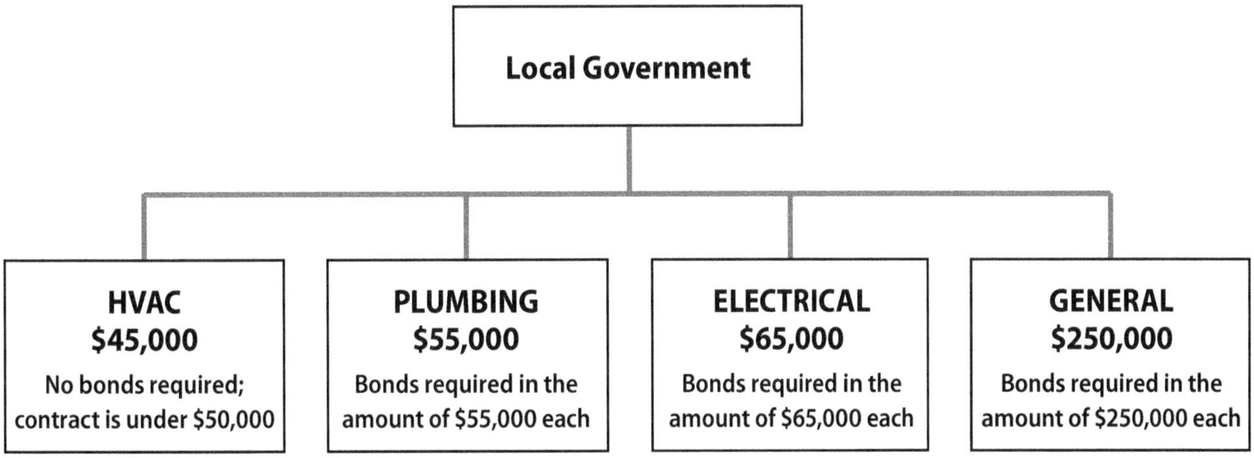

Figure 2.4 Requirements for Performance and Payment Bonds under Single-Prime Contracting

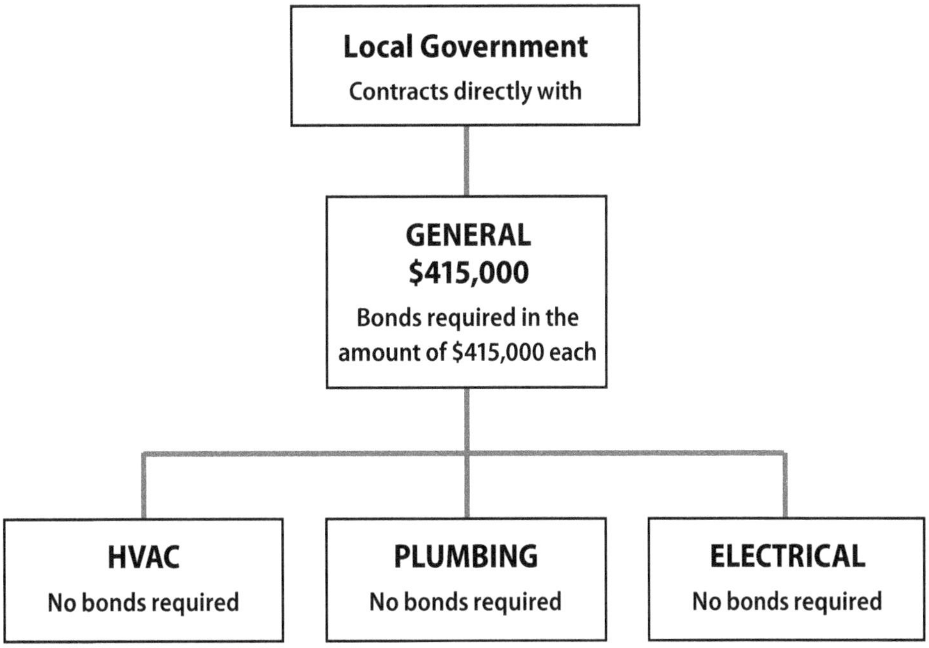

or she forfeits the bid deposit. If a public official or employee who is responsible for obtaining performance and payment bonds does not do so, that official or employee is guilty of a Class 1 misdemeanor.[40]

Performance and payment bonds must be provided by each contractor who has a contract *directly* with the local government. The charts in Figures 2.3 and 2.4 illustrate the type of contracts for which performance and payment bonds are required.

---

40. G.S. 44A-32.

In the first example (Figure 2.3), with a total project cost of $415,000 (the sum of all four contracts entered into directly with the unit of government), no bonds are required for the HVAC contract because it is below the $50,000 threshold. Bonds are required for the plumbing, electrical, and general contracts, however, because each exceeds the $50,000 threshold. In the second example (Figure 2.4), the total project cost is also $415,000, but because the contract was entered into between the general contractor and the unit of government, the subcontractors are not contracting directly with the local government and therefore are not subject to performance and payment bond requirements.

The specific requirements for performance and payment bonds on public construction contracts are governed under Article 3 of Chapter 44A. Often referred to as the "Little Miller Act," Article 3 is modeled after the federal Miller Act, which requires performance and payment bonds on certain federal construction projects.[41] Model bond provisions can be found in G.S. 44A-33. In addition to the projects for which performance and payment bonds are mandated under Article 3, the local government also may, at its discretion, require performance and payment bonds for smaller contracts.

2.72. What is a performance bond?

A performance bond protects the local government by securing the contractor's "faithful performance of the contract in accordance with the plans, specifications and conditions of the contract" and is solely for the protection of the local government (the contracting entity).[42] It provides a remedy for the local government in the event the contractor does not complete the project or otherwise does not fully perform under the contract. The performance bond must be 100 percent of the contract amount.

2.73. What is a payment bond?

A payment bond protects subcontractors and suppliers that furnish materials or labor on a construction project by ensuring prompt payment by the contractor or subcontractor who is liable for the payment. The payment bond is solely for the protection of subcontractors and suppliers who furnish such labor or materials.[43] Like the performance bond, the payment bond must be 100 percent of the construction contract amount.

2.74. What form must the bonds be in, and what information must they contain?

To ensure compliance with Chapter 44A, Article 3, performance and payment bond forms must contain

- the date the bond is executed;
- the names of the principal (contractor), surety, and contracting body (local government);
- the amount of the bond (for payment bonds, this requirement is inferred from various provisions of Article 3);
- the contract number; and
- appropriate places for the surety and principal to execute (sign) the bond. In the case of a corporate body, the bond must be executed under seal, with the corporate seal affixed to the bond and the bond signed by the corporation's representative acting pursuant to authority of its governing body.[44]

The bonds also must contain a number of conditions set out in G.S. 44A-33(a) (performance bonds) or G.S. 44A-33(b) (payment bonds). For example, both G.S. 44A-33(a) and (b) specify that "any and all duly authorized modifications" that may be made in the contract are covered by the bond and that notice of contract modifications is waived by the surety.

---

41. 40 U.S.C. §§ 3131–34.
42. G.S. 44A-26(a)(1).
43. G.S. 44A-26(a)(2).
44. G.S. 44A-33(a) & (b).

Performance and payment bonds given to a local government must be executed by one or more surety companies legally authorized to do business in North Carolina.[45] However, as is the case with bid bonds, the local government or anyone acting on its behalf may not require a contractor to procure a performance or payment bond from *any particular* surety, agent, producer, or broker as long as the North Carolina licensure requirement is met.[46] If a surety is North Carolina–licensed, the local government is probably required to allow the contractor to use it, even if the local government may have concerns about the surety's financial condition. The local government should raise these financial issues with the surety's licensing agency, the North Carolina Department of Insurance.

There is one situation in which the bond of a North Carolina–licensed surety *may* be rejected. As noted in section II.C.4 of this chapter, the local government may reject a surety company's bond if there is an unsettled state or local governmental contractual claim or complaint against the company that has been pending for more than 180 days.[47]

2.75. What if there is a technical defect in the bond forms? Can we still accept it?

G.S. 44A-30(b) stipulates that performance and payment bonds given by a contractor under that article are "conclusively presumed" to have been given in accordance with the provisions of that article, even if the bonds are not drawn to meet its requirements. This statute also stipulates that it is "conclusively presumed" that Article 3 has been written into every bond given pursuant to it.[48]

This presumption means that while the interested parties—the local government, the contractor, and the surety—must comply with the bond statutes, they may not use technical defects in a performance or payment bond as grounds for setting it aside.

2.76. Can we require a deposit in lieu of bonds?

Yes. In lieu of requiring payment and performance bonds, a local government may require the contractor to make a deposit of money, certified check, or government securities for the full amount of the contract "to secure the faithful performance of the terms of [the] contract and the payment of all sums due for labor and materials in a manner consistent with Article 3 of Chapter 44A."[49] In the unlikely event[50] that a contractor makes such a deposit in lieu of posting bonds, the board or governing body that receives the deposit "assumes all the liabilities, obligations and duties of a surety as provided in Article 3 of Chapter 44A to the extent of said deposit." Because the statute requires that the deposit cover the full amount of the contract, the amount of the deposit should be increased any time a change order increases the amount of the contract.

Although the statute does not specifically require separate deposits to secure both performance and payment, because the statute references Article 3 of Chapter 44A, which does specifically require separate bonds, each of which must be 100 percent of the contract amount, the deposits should mirror the bond requirement. Thus if a local government requires deposits in lieu of posting bonds, it must secure two separate deposits from the contractor, and each deposit must be for 100 percent of the contract amount.

The statutes do not say who is entitled to the interest earned on amounts deposited with the board or governing body in lieu of posting bonds. Unless the board specifies otherwise, however, the interest presumably belongs to the contractor since it is the contractor's money that is being held. The board would be wise to settle this question in advance through a provision in the project specifications.

---

45. G.S. 44A-26. In some instances it may be necessary to verify that the surety's representative who executes the bond has the authority to act on its behalf. The North Carolina Department of Insurance or the Secretary of State's Office can assist the local government in answering this question directly or in contacting the surety company to obtain an answer, if there is any concern.

46. G.S. 58-31-66(a).

47. G.S. 143-129(c).

48. *Applied in* Pyco Supply Co. v. Am. Centennial Ins. Co., 321 N.C. 435 (1988) (payment bond).

49. G.S. 143-129(c).

50. In practice, it would be unusual for a contractor to tie up the large amount of capital required for a deposit.

2.77. Can a letter of credit serve in the place of a bond?

No. Sometimes a contractor may ask to provide the local government with a letter of credit from a financial institution in lieu of providing bonds or one of the forms of deposit set out above. However, the use of letters of credit is not authorized for construction and repair projects covered by the formal bidding statute. Only the four forms of security listed in question 2.15 are permissible.

2.78. Can the amount of the bonds be adjusted or modified?

The contractor, surety, and contracting body may not *reduce* or limit the contractor's or surety's liability as set out in Article 3 of Chapter 44A, which is 100 percent of the construction contract amount for each bond.[51] However, if the amount of the contract is increased (such as through a change order), the amount of both bonds should be increased by the corresponding amount. Bonds are often written so that such an increase occurs automatically.

2.79. When do the bonds become effective, and how long do they remain in effect?

The bonds become effective when the construction or repair contract is awarded and must remain in effect throughout the life of the project.[52]

2.80. What if the contractor fails to provide performance and payment bonds?

A contractor who fails to provide "satisfactory surety," meaning satisfactory performance and payment bonds, forfeits his or her bid deposit. Since the bonds become effective when the contract is awarded and work on the project should not commence until the bonds have been provided, the local government should require the contractor to provide the bonds as soon as possible thereafter.

2.81. May we require performance and payment bonds on projects other than those required by statute?

Yes. The local government may choose to require a contractor to furnish performance and payment bonds for projects costing less than $300,000, or if the project exceeds $300,000, on contracts for that project costing less than $50,000. When considering whether to require performance and payment bonds beyond what is required by statute, the local government should bear in mind the additional cost incurred by the contractor in securing these bonds, a cost that likely will be passed on to the unit of government in the contractor's bid price.

III. Informal Bidding Procedures

Construction or repair contracts involving the expenditure of $30,000 or more but less than $500,000 of public funds are subject to informal bidding requirements.[53] Note that it is the size of the *contract*, not the size of the *project*, that determines whether informal bidding is allowed. For example, a $660,000 project might involve several contracts, each worth less than $500,000. In this instance, the local government is permitted to use informal bidding procedures for each contract.

2.82. What if the good faith estimate of the project is under $500,000 but one or more of the bids exceeds $500,000? Can we still award the contract?

It is important to note that informal bidding procedures apply to the *actual* cost of the contract, not its *estimated* cost, as is the case under the formal bidding statutes. Because local governments cannot award a construction or repair contract in the formal bidding range unless it has complied with the formal bidding requirements, the local government could award a contract using informal bidding procedures only if the winning bid is less than

51. G.S. 44A-30(a).

52. G.S. 44A-26. *See* James River Equip., Inc. v. Tharpe's Excavating, Inc., 179 N.C. App. 336, 342 (2006).

53. G.S. 143-131. Competitive bids are not required at all if the cost of the contract is less than $30,000, unless the local government chooses to set a threshold that is lower than the statutory thresholds at which it will require informal or formal bidding.

$500,000 because the *actual* cost of the contract is in the informal bidding range. Otherwise, the local government must rebid the project following the formal bidding requirement.

2.83. What are the informal bidding requirements?

The informal bidding statute sets out only minimal procedural requirements. Specifically, the local government must

1. "secure" bids,
2. keep a record of all bids received,
3. award the contract to the lowest responsive, responsible bidder.

In addition, if the construction or repair project involves a building, the local government must engage in informal HUB recruitment efforts, namely, solicit HUB participation, maintain a record of HUB firms solicited, and document its HUB participation recruitment efforts (see Chapter 4 for further discussion of HUB requirements).[54]

2.84. Can we include some or all of the formal bidding requirements in our informal bidding procedures?

Yes. Although not required to do so by statute, local governments may opt to utilize some or all of the formal bidding procedures in an informal bidding process. If it chooses to do so, the local government should clearly state all such requirements in its bid solicitation documents.

2.85. What form of advertising is required?

The informal bidding statute only requires the local government to "secure" bids. No specific method of advertisement is required, including formal newspaper advertisement. Thus local governments may solicit bids through a variety of methods, including posting the bid notice on its website, emailing its bidders list, and calling potential bidders.

2.86. Must informal bids be received sealed?

No. The informal bidding statute does not require bids to be submitted sealed. For this reason, bid documents and the record of bids do not become subject to public inspection until the contract has been awarded.[55]

2.87. In what form may informal bids be received?

Unlike formal bids, informal bids may be received in any form—paper, fax, email, even oral quotes given over the phone. It is because of the informality with which these bids may be received that the statute requires the local government to keep a record of bids.

2.88. Do we have to receive three bids in order to award a contract?

No. The three-bid minimum requirement applies only to construction and repair contracts in the formal bidding range. Although the informal bidding statute does not specify a minimum number of bids that must be received in order to award a contract, the statute does refer to bids in the plural, meaning that the local government should make a good faith effort to secure at least two bids. However, if two bids are not secured, the local government is not prohibited from awarding the contract. Some local governments impose the three-bid minimum requirement on informal bids under their local procurement policies; if this is the case, the local government must follow its own policies.

2.89. What information must be included in the record of bids?

While the informal bidding statute does not specify the form or content of the record of bids, it is recommended that the record of bids indicate the name of the project (and project number if applicable), the date on which bids were received, the name of the bidders, and the bid amounts. Because informal bids are subject to the same lowest

---

54. G.S. 143-131(b).

55. For an excellent discussion of the application of the public records laws to bid documents see Eileen Youens, *When Are Bids and Proposals Subject to Public Inspection?* Local Gov't L. Bull. No. 119 (Feb. 2009), http://sogpubs.unc.edu/electronicversions/pdfs/lglb119.pdf.

Informal and Formal Competitive Bidding Requirements for Construction and Repair Projects

Bidding Requirements	Informal ($30,000–$500,000)	Formal ($500,000 and above)
Solicitation advertisement	No specific method required; local government may choose to "secure" bids by any means	Formal notice published in newspaper for 7 days between date of publication and bid opening; may also use electronic means in addition to newspaper (electronic means only requires governing board approval)
Form of bids	Any form; must keep record of bids	Bids must be sealed and in paper form
Number of bids received		At least 3
Bid bond	Not Required	Must be submitted with bid; must equal at least 5% of bid amount
Bid deadline	No statutory deadline	Bid must be received by date and time of bid opening
HUB requirements	Must solicit HUB participation and document recruitment efforts	Formal HUB requirements for local governments and bidders
Public bid opening	Not required	Required
Standard of award	Lowest responsive, responsible bidder	Lowest responsive, responsible bidder
Board approval	Not required	Required
Public record	Record of bids not public until contract awarded	Bids become public when opened

responsive, responsible bidder standard of award as are formal bids, the record of bids should also include sufficient information to justify the local government's contract award decision in the event of a legal challenge.

The record of bids should not be viewed as a substitute for the contract document executed with the bidding bidder. While the contract may be in simplified form, such as an invoice, the local government must still ensure that all necessary terms and conditions are included.

2.90. Are bid bonds required?

No. Bid bonds are required by law only for construction and repair contracts in the formal bidding range. However, a local government may choose to require a bid bond if it determines that such is in its best interest. If it does so, it should clearly state this requirement in its bid solicitation documents.

2.91. If we require a bid bond and the lowest bidder does not submit one, can we waive that defect?

No. Although not statutorily required to do so for informal bids, a local government must adhere to its own local purchasing policies and the conditions it places on the bidding process. Keeping in mind when deviations or defects in bids may be waived under the lowest responsive, responsible bidder standard of award, the local government is not permitted to waive a material variance. Because obtaining a bid bond involves both time and expense on the part of the bidder, waiving this variance would give that bidder an unfair competitive advantage over other bidders who complied with this requirement.

2.92. Are performance and payment bonds required?

Performance and payment bond requirements apply even if the cost of the contracts awarded for the project fall within the informal bidding range. Thus performance and payment bonds are required for each contract with the local government costing $50,000 or more on projects where the total cost of all contracts for the project exceeds $300,000 (see section II.H.2 of this chapter for further discussion of performance and payment bond requirements).

The local government may choose to impose performance and payment bonds on contracts below the statutory threshold; if it does, it should make bidders aware of this requirement during the bid solicitation process.

2.93. What is the standard of award for informal contracts?

Informal contracts must be awarded to the lowest responsive, responsible bidder, which is the same standard of award that applies to formal contracts (see section II.F of this chapter for further discussion of the standard of award).

2.94. Who is authorized to award and execute informal contracts?

Unlike with construction and repair contracts in the formal bidding range, governing board approval is not statutorily required for the award of informal contracts. Nor do the bidding statutes stipulate who is authorized to execute the contract. Consequently, any employee or official who has the authority to legally bind a unit of government may award and execute the contract.

2.95. What is the time frame within which an informal contract must be executed?

While the formal bidding statutes require a successful bidder to execute the contract within ten days of award or risk forfeiture of the bid bond, no similar requirement applies to informal contracts.

IV. Prequalification

Prequalification of bidders for public construction contracts is expressly authorized by statute under specific circumstances. G.S. 143-135.8 provides general authorization for prequalification of bidders on construction and repair projects, and G.S. 143-128.1(a) deals specifically with prequalification when the "construction management at-risk" contracting method is used. (This method is discussed in section VIII.A of Chapter 3.)

A. Definition of Prequalification

Prequalification is defined as a "process of evaluating and determining whether potential bidders have the skill, judgment, integrity, sufficient financial resources, and ability necessary to the faithful performance of a contract for construction or repair work."[56] This statutory definition mirrors the definition of a responsible bidder articulated by the North Carolina Court of Appeals that applies to the lowest responsive, responsible bidder standard of award for contracts in the informal and formal competitive bidding ranges.[57] Thus the legal standard for prequalification is the same as that for determining whether a bidder is responsible.

Practically speaking, when a local government uses prequalification in a bidding process it conducts some aspects of its responsible bidder determination *prior* to receiving bids instead of when considering bids *after* they have been received. The local government first prequalifies potential bidders and then receives bids only from them. The local government may still apply the responsible bidder standard when evaluating bids, but it may not reject a bidder as being not responsible based on a specific factor on which the local government granted prequalification for bidding on that contract.

---

56. G.S. 143-135.8(f)(2).

57. Kinsey Contracting Co. v. City of Fayetteville, 106 N.C. App. 383, 385, *disc. review denied*, 332 N.C. 345 (1992).

B. When Prequalification May Be Used

Under G.S. 143-135.8, prequalification of bidders for construction and repair contracts is prohibited unless the requirements of this statute are followed.[58] Prequalification may be used when *all* of the following conditions are met:

(a) The local government is using one of the construction methods authorized in G.S. 143-128(a1)(1) through -128(a1)(3) (single-prime, separate-prime, or dual-bidding; see sections VII.A–C of Chapter 3 for a discussion of these construction methods).
(b) The board or governing body adopts an objective prequalification policy applicable to all construction or repair work; the policy must be adopted prior to the advertisement of the contract for which the governmental entity intends to prequalify bidders.
(c) The local government has adopted the assessment tool and criteria for that specific project, which must include the prequalification scoring values and minimum required score for prequalification on that project.[59]

Prequalification is specifically prohibited when selecting architects, engineers, surveyors, construction managers at-risk, design-builders, preliminary designers for design-build bridging projects, and private developers for public-private partnership contracts (see sections VIII.A–D of Chapter 3 and Chapter 7).

C. Dollar Threshold

The statute does not set a dollar threshold or minimum contract cost for when prequalification may be used. While prequalification can be used only when a local government employs the single-prime, separate-prime, or dual-bidding contracting methods, local governments are not prohibited from using these methods for other types of construction projects in addition to building construction projects costing $300,000 or more. Thus local governments are authorized to prequalify contractors on any construction or repair project bid using the single-prime, separate-prime, or dual-bidding methods, regardless of the type of project or its cost.

D. Prequalification Criteria Policy

The prequalification statute specifically requires that a local government's prequalification criteria policy must

(a) be uniform, consistent, and transparent in its application to all bidders;
(b) allow all bidders who meet the prequalification criteria to be prequalified to bid on the construction or repair work project;
(c) clearly state the prequalification criteria, which must comply with all of the following:
    i. be rationally related to construction or repair work,
    ii. not require that the bidder has previously been awarded a construction or repair project by the governmental entity,
    iii. permit bidders to submit history or experience with projects of similar size, scope, or complexity;
(d) clearly state the assessment process of the criteria to be used;
(e) establish a process for a denied bidder to protest to the governmental entity denial of prequalification, which process shall be completed prior to the opening of bids under G.S. 143-129(b) and which allows sufficient time for a bidder subsequently prequalified pursuant to a protest to submit a bid on the contract for which the bidder is subsequently prequalified;
(f) outline a process by which the basis for denial of prequalification will be communicated in writing, upon request, to a bidder who is denied prequalification.

---

58. G.S. 143-135.8(a).
59. G.S. 143-135.8(b).

E. Notice to Bidders of Prequalification

Although G.S. 143-135.8 does not require a specific method of notice to bidders that prequalification is being used as part of the contracting process for a particular project, a local government should include notice of prequalification in whatever notice for the opportunity to submit bids is given (for example, in the legal advertisement required under formal bidding procedures). In lieu of giving notice of prequalification in the initial bid solicitation notice, a local government could choose to issue two notices—the first giving notice of the opportunity to submit qualifications and the second giving notice of the date, time, and location of the public bid opening (if the project is subject to formal bidding requirements). Regardless of the method used for giving notice of prequalification, a local government should make available its prequalification criteria policy, criteria, and assessment tool to ensure that interested bidders are able to fully comply with the local government's requirements for submitting qualifications.

F. Prequalification Denial Protest Procedure

Local governments are required to establish in their prequalification policies a process by which a contractor who has been denied prequalification may protest that denial.[60] The protest procedure must be completed prior to the bid opening and allow sufficient time for a contractor whose protest is successful (i.e., the contractor is subsequently granted prequalification as a result of the protest) to submit a bid on the project. Beyond these two requirements, the statute provides no other guidance on the structure of the protest procedures, leaving to a local government's discretion such matters as the time frame in which a contractor must file the protest, whether the protest must be in writing, who will review and make a decision on the protest, the time frame within which a decision will be rendered, and whether there will be an opportunity to appeal the decision if unfavorable. However the process is to be structured, local governments should articulate their process as clearly as possible. For example, if a contractor is given three days in which to submit a protest, the policy should state whether those days are calendar days or business days.

Local governments must take into account the protest process when setting the bid deadline. As stated above, the prequalification statute requires that the protest procedure be structured to allow sufficient time for a contractor who is subsequently granted prequalification to submit a bid on the project. A bid deadline that follows too closely the conclusion of a protest process will not enable a subsequently prequalified contractor to put together a competitive bid package and also will disadvantage subcontractors who may wish to submit bids to that contractor.

It is particularly important to allow sufficient time between the conclusion of the protest procedure and the bid deadline on projects subject to formal historically underutilized business (HUB) requirements (building construction projects with an estimated cost of $300,000 or greater are subject to formal HUB requirements; see Chapter 4 for further discussion). Among the good faith efforts available to bidders under formal HUB requirements is contacting minority businesses to submit a quote at least ten days before the bid deadline.[61] Similarly, local governments are required to provide notice to HUB contractors and subcontractors of the opportunity to bid and certain information about the project at least ten days prior to the bid deadline.[62] Local governments must take into account these time frames when setting the bid deadline to ensure that the prequalification protest process is completed in sufficient time to allow both the local government and a contractor subsequently granted prequalification to comply with HUB requirements.

---

60. G.S. 143-135.8(c)(5).
61. G.S. 143-128.2(f)(1).
62. G.S. 143-128.2(e)(3).

G. Bids from Bidders Who Are Not Prequalified

The prequalification statute specifically states that a bid submitted by a bidder who was not prequalified "shall" be rejected as being nonresponsive.[63] However, as discussed above, the local government is required to accept a bid from a bidder who was initially denied prequalification and then subsequently prequalified after filing a protest under the local government's prequalification policy.

V. Bid Protest Procedures

Unlike the laws governing state and federal contracting, North Carolina laws governing local government contracting do not require or establish bid protest procedures. North Carolina courts have held that if a contract is subject to the statutory competitive bidding procedures and those procedures are not followed, the contract is void.[64] If a bidder is dissatisfied with a decision of the local government—for example, to award a contract to the second-lowest bidder or to accept a bid that does not meet specifications—the bidder can register his or her complaint with the local official responsible for the contract or register it directly with the governing board. As a practical matter, it is best for the unit to attempt to resolve the matter, but there is no legal requirement for a hearing or other formal disposition of the complaint. If the matter is not resolved administratively, the only legal option is for the aggrieved party to sue the unit of government, typically for an injunction to prevent the unit from going forward with an illegal contract.[65] It is not unusual for protests to be lodged with local government officials or with governing boards, though legal challenges are rare.

Although a bid protest procedure is not required under state law, local governments must, in most instances, provide a settlement process for disappointed bidders on projects funded in whole or in part with federal grant funds.[66]

---

63. G.S. 143-135.8(d).

64. Raynor v. Comm'rs of Louisburg, 220 N.C. 348, 353 (1941).

65. *See* Frayda S. Bluestein, *Disappointed Bidder Claims against North Carolina Local Governments*, LOCAL GOV'T L. BULL. No. 98 (May 2001), www.sogpubs.unc.edu/electronicversions/pdfs/lglb98.pdf.

66. This requirement is found under subsections .36(b)(11) and (12) of the Grants Management Common Rule.

Appendix 2A Dollar Thresholds in North Carolina Public Contracting Statutes

Requirement	Threshold	Statute
Formal bidding	*(estimated cost of contract)*	
Construction or repair contracts	$500,000 *and above*	G.S. 143-129
Purchase of apparatus, supplies, materials, and equipment	$90,000 *and above*	G.S. 143-129
Informal bidding	*(actual cost of contract)*	
Construction or repair contracts	$30,000 to formal limit	G.S. 143-131
Purchase of apparatus, supplies, materials, and equipment	$30,000 to formal limit	G.S. 143-131
Construction methods authorized for building projects	*Over* $300,000	G.S. 143-128(a1)
Separate Prime	*(estimated cost of project)*	
Single Prime		
Dual Bidding		
Construction Management at Risk *(G.S. 143-128.1)*		
Design-Build and Design-Build Bridging *(G.S. 143-128.1A; G.S. 143-128.1B)*		
Public-Private Partnership (P3) *(G.S. 143-128.1C)*		
Historically Underutilized Business (HUB) requirements		
Building construction or repair projects		
– Projects with state funding *(verifiable 10% goal required)*	$100,000 *or more*	G.S. 143-128.2(a)
– Locally funded projects *(formal HUB requirements)*	$300,000 *or more*	G.S. 143-128.2(j)
– Projects in informal bidding range *(informal HUB requirements)*	$30,000 to $500,000*	G.S. 143-131(b)
**Note: Formal HUB requirements should be used for informally bid projects costing between $300,000 and $500,000*		
Limit on use of own forces (force account work)	*(not to exceed)*	G.S. 143-135
Construction or repair projects	$125,000 *(total project cost)* or $50,000 *(labor only cost)*	
Bid bond or deposit		
Construction or repair contracts *(at least 5% of bid amount)*	Formal bids *($500,000 and above)*	G.S. 143-129(b)
Purchase contracts	Not required	
Performance/Payment bonds		
Construction or repair contracts *(100% of contract amount)*	Each contract *over* $50,000 of project costing *over* $300,000	G.S. 143-129(c); G.S. 44A-26
Purchase contracts	Not required	
General contractor's license required	$30,000 *and above*	G.S. 87-1
Exemption	Force account work *(see above)*	
Owner-builder affidavit required	Force account work *(see above)*	G.S. 87-14(a)(1)
Use of licensed architect or engineer required		
Nonstructural work	$300,000 *and above*	G.S. 133-1.1(a)
Structural repair, additions, or new construction	$135,000 *and above*	
Repair work affecting life safety systems	$100,000 *and above*	
Selection of architect, engineer, surveyor, construction manager at risk, or design-build contractor		
"Qualification-Based Selection" procedure (QBS)	All contracts unless exempted	G.S. 143-64.31
Exemption authorized	Only projects where estimated fee is *less than* $50,000	G.S. 143-64.32

Dollar limits and statutory authority current as of September 1, 2013. From *A Legal Guide to Purchasing and Contracting for North Carolina Local Governments*, 2nd ed., by Frayda S. Bluestein,

Appendix 2B Awarding Competitively Bid Contracts: Lowest Responsive, Responsible Bidder Flowchart

Lowest Cost: Determine which bid has the lowest proposed cost.

↓

Responsive Bid: Is lowest bid responsive?

✓ Bid meets applicable **legal requirements**.

✓ Bid **conforms "substantially"** to the bid specifications.

Note: If the bid does not conform completely to the specifications, ask if it's fair to the other bidders to waive the defect/irregularity:

- Would waiving the defect/irregularity give the bidder an **advantage** over the other bidders?
- Would other bidders **change their bids** if they could use the same defect/irregularity?

If no unfair competitive advantage, the bid conforms "substantially" to the specifications.

→ If low bid is not responsive, **reject** and evaluate second lowest bid to determine if it is responsive. If second lowest bid is not responsive, **reject** this bid and **repeat** with third lowest bidder, and so on.

↓

Responsible Bidder: Is lowest bidder responsible, considering the **quality**, **performance** and the **time specified** for performance in the bidder's proposal?

✓ Bidder has the **skill**, **judgment**, and **integrity** necessary to faithfully perform the contract.

✓ Bidder has sufficient **financial resources** to perform the contract.

✓ Bidder has the **ability** to perform the contract.

→ If low bid is responsive but the bidder is not responsible, **reject** and evaluate second lowest bid to determine if it is responsive and the bidder is responsible. If not, **reject** this bid and **repeat** with third lowest bidder, and so on.

↓

If lowest bid is responsive and lowest bidder is responsible, you may **recommend awarding** the contract to this bidder.

Note: If the cost of the bid is in excess of funds available and bidder agrees to negotiate, may negotiate with bidder to bring within budget so long as scope of project is not substantially modified (G.S. 143-129(b)).

Sources: G.S. 143-128, -129, -131; Prof'l Food Servs. Mgmt. v. N.C. Dep't of Admin., 109 N.C. App. 265 (1993); Kinsey Contracting Co. v. City of Fayetteville, 106 N.C. App. 383, *disc. review denied*, 332 N.C. 345 (1992). For additional information see Frayda S. Bluestein, *Understanding the Responsiveness Requirement in Competitive Bidding*, Local Gov't L. Bull. No. 102 (May 2002), www.sog.unc.edu/pubs/electronicversions/pdfs/lglb102.pdf.

Chapter 3

Construction and Repair Projects Involving Buildings

Chapter 3

Construction and Repair Projects Involving Buildings

I. Introduction

Beyond the competitive bidding requirements discussed in Chapter 2, projects that involve the erection, construction, alteration, or repair of a *building* or *buildings* have additional bidding requirements, especially those with an estimated cost greater than $300,000.

Note that the $300,000 threshold that triggers additional bidding requirements for building construction projects is lower than the $500,000 threshold for formal bidding requirements. Thus, while construction or repair projects with an estimated cost of between $300,000 and $500,000 may be contracted using informal bidding procedures, the additional bidding requirements discussed in this chapter still apply. For this reason, many local governments will use formal bidding procedures for construction or repair projects involving buildings where the estimated cost is $300,000.

Additional building construction contract requirements are triggered at $300,000, as illustrated in Figure 3.1.

II. What Is a Building?

The North Carolina General Statutes (hereinafter G.S.) do not define the term *building* for the purposes of competitive bidding requirements. In the absence of a statutory definition, the term's plain and ordinary meaning applies.[1] *Webster's* defines a building (noun, not verb) as "a roofed and walled structure built for permanent use."[2] The North Carolina Court of Appeals has looked to *Black's Law Dictionary* in defining a building as a "[s]tructure designed for habitation, shelter, storage, trade, manufacture, religion, business, education, and the like. A structure or edifice inclosing a space within its walls, and usually, but not necessarily, covered with a roof."[3]

Though not exclusively, the word building is usually associated with construction projects that require plumbing as well as heating, ventilation, and air conditioning (HVAC) contractors. Most jurisdictions interpret building construction and repair to mean that the requirements do not apply to other types of construction, such as streets or utilities. Sometimes the particular nature of a construction or repair project can cause confusion over whether

---

1. State v. Wiggins, 272 N.C. 147, 153 (1967), *cert. denied*, 390 U.S. 1028 (1968); State v. Felts, 79 N.C. App. 205, 208, *disc. review denied*, 316 N.C. 555 (1986).

2. Merriam-Webster's Collegiate Dictionary (10th ed. 2002).

3. Davidson Cnty. v. City of High Point, 85 N.C. App. 26, 38, *aff'd and modified*, 321 N.C. 252 (1987) (quoting Black's Law Dictionary 176 (5th ed. 1979)).

Figure 3.1 Additional Building Construction Requirements Are Triggered for Building Construction Contracts Costing $300,000 and Above

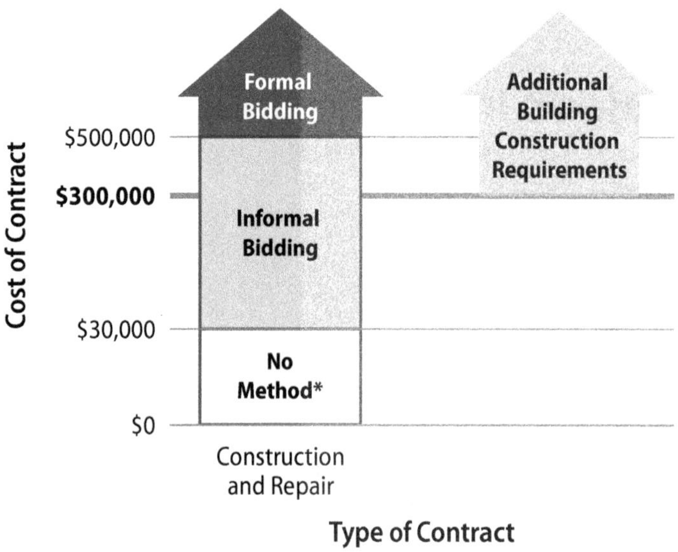

*Local governments may impose lower bid thresholds by local policy

the structure involved is actually a building. For example, a gazebo has a roof but no walls; is it a building? Under Webster's definition, the answer is no. When in doubt, it is safer to follow the more stringent statutory requirements that apply to building construction and repair projects to ensure the validity of the contract in the event of a legal challenge.

The building construction statute does exempt certain structures from the requirements that apply to large building construction or repair projects (those costing more than $300,000). The purchase and erection of prefabricated or re-locatable buildings, such as office trailers, are not covered under the large building construction requirements.[4] However, any work that must be performed at the site is not included within this exemption, meaning that on-site construction work is subject not only to competitive bidding requirements but also to the additional requirements for building construction if a building other than the prefabricated one is involved.

III. Summary of Building Construction Contracting Requirements

The requirements that apply to bidding and contracting for construction or repair work involving a building are summarized in Table 3.1.

In addition to the requirements outlined above, the plans and specifications for certain building and construction repair projects are subject to additional statutory requirements depending on the size and nature of the project and its cost. These requirements (discussed in section IX, below) include the requirement that plans and specifications be drawn by a licensed architect or engineer and approved by the state commissioner of insurance for fire safety.

4. Section 143-128(g)(1) of the North Carolina General Statutes (hereinafter G.S.). The purchase of a prefabricated or re-locatable building would still be subject to the competitive bidding requirements that apply to purchase contracts under either G.S. 143-131 (informal bidding) or G.S. 143-129 (formal bidding). In addition, general contractor licensure requirements and dispute resolution procedures will still apply.

Table 3.1 Summary of Additional Building Construction and Repair Contracting Requirements

Requirement	Below $30,000	$30,000–$300,000	Over $300,000
Dispute resolution procedures	✓	✓	✓
Separate specifications			✓
Specific bidding and delivery methods (traditional and alternative)			✓
HUB requirements[a]		✓	✓

a. See Chapter 4 for a discussion of HUB requirements.

IV. Dispute Resolution Requirement

For all building construction and repair projects, regardless of cost (even projects costing less than $30,000), a local government must adopt and provide for a dispute resolution process.[5] The purpose of this process is to provide a means by which those involved in the construction project can resolve disputes or issues arising from the project before resorting to litigation. In fact, the local government may require in its contracts that a party participate in mediation before initiating litigation. The dispute resolution process must be made available to all parties involved in the construction project, including the local government, architects and engineers, contractors, and subcontractors. In addition, the dispute resolution process must include an opportunity for mediation. To avoid having the process used to resolve nominal disputes, the local government may set a minimum amount in controversy of up to $15,000. Local governments may choose to adopt their own dispute resolution procedures (which must include mediation), or they may adopt those adopted by the State Building Commission.[6]

A dispute resolution process should not be confused with claims made against the contractor's performance or payment bonds. The specific components of a dispute resolution process and claims made against bonds are discussed in sections III and V of Chapter 6. In addition, the dispute resolution process is available only to those entities under contract with the local government for the construction project; it is not available for use by disappointed bidders who wish to protest the local government's contract award decision (bid protest procedures are not required under state law but are required as a condition of receiving most federal grant funds for construction work; see section V of Chapter 2).

V. Separate Specifications Requirement

For all building projects where the cost of the project exceeds $300,000, separate specifications must be drawn for each of four subdivisions or branches of construction work.[7] These branches or subdivisions, which are commonly thought of in terms of the specific licensure requirements associated with each, are

1. *HVAC*—heating, ventilating, air conditioning, and accessories (separately or combined into one conductive system), refrigeration for cold storage (where the cold storage cooling load is fifteen tons or more of refrigeration), and all related work;
2. *Plumbing*—plumbing and gas fittings and accessories and all related work;
3. *Electrical*—electrical wiring and installations and all related work;

5. G.S. 143-128(f1).

6. The dispute resolution procedures adopted by the State Building Commission are available on the State Construction Office website, www.nc-sco.com/guidelines.aspx.

7. G.S. 143-128(a).

4. *General*—general work relating to the erection, construction, alteration, or repair of any building that is not included in the first three branches (this work typically requires the contractor to be licensed as a general contractor).

Local governments may, at their option, prepare specifications for other categories of work besides those listed above. But, at a minimum, at least four sets of specifications must be drawn.

If the project is being bid using the separate-prime bidding method (see section VII.A, below) and estimated cost of the work in one of the four branches is less than $25,000, that work may be included in the specifications for one of the other branches. For example, a renovation project might involve $350,000 of general work and $20,000 of electrical work. In that case, if the local government is using the separate-prime bidding method, the specifications for the electrical work could be combined with the general work specifications.

VI. Summary of Large Building Bidding and Construction Delivery Methods

Local governments have a variety of options for construction delivery methods when bidding building construction projects costing more than $300,000. While specifically authorized for large building construction projects, these bidding and delivery methods also may be used for construction and repair projects that do not involve buildings, such as utilities upgrades or street paving. Because all of these bidding and construction delivery methods are statutorily authorized (and, in fact, are required for large building construction projects), local governments are free to choose which specific option will best suit its needs on a particular project.

For purposes of this chapter, the authorized bidding and construction delivery options have been divided into two categories—traditional and alternative. Within each category are the options authorized by statute.[8]

1. Traditional methods include
   a. separate-prime (sometimes referred to as multiple-prime),
   b. single-prime,
   c. dual-bidding.
2 Alternative methods include
   a. construction management at-risk,
   b. design-build,
   c. design-build bridging,
   d. public-private partnerships,
   e. alternative contracting methods approved by the State Building Commission or the General Assembly (through a local act).

VII. Traditional Bidding and Construction Delivery Methods

A. Separate-Prime (Multiple-Prime) Bidding

For many years, separate—or multiple-prime—bidding and contracting was the only contracting method allowed by statute for state agencies and local governments for many years, and it remains a viable option. Under this system, the local government advertises for and receives separate bids for each of the four categories of branches or subdivisions of work for which separate specifications must be prepared (HVAC, plumbing, electrical, and general), and a separate contract is awarded for each of the listed branches of work.[9] Because at least four sets of

8 G.S. 143-128(a1).
9. G.S. 143-128(b).

Figure 3.2 Separate-Prime/(Multiple-Prime) Bidding Method

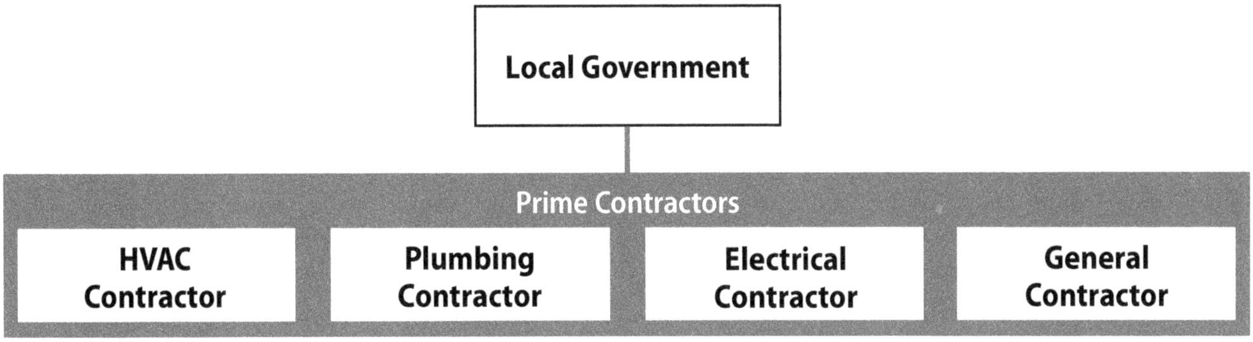

specifications must be drawn (see section V, above), the local government will have at least four contractors with whom it contracts directly (making these contractors prime contractors).

Each prime contractor is directly liable to both the local government and the other contractors for fully performing its contractual duties and obligations in accordance with the plans and specifications. This obligation applies to all individuals who and businesses that contract directly with the local government.

The separate-prime (multiple-prime) bidding method is illustrated in Figure 3.2. In evaluating bids and awarding contracts under the separate-prime method, the local government applies the lowest responsive, responsible bidder standard of award in each of the categories of work for which it has solicited bids (as described above, there will always be at least four categories of work). As with all construction and repair contracts subject to competitive bidding requirements, this standard of award applies to projects in both the formal and informal bidding ranges. However, the bidding procedures themselves may vary depending on the estimated cost of the contract under each category of work. As discussed in section I.C of Chapter 2, since informal and formal competitive bidding requirements apply to the cost of the *contract*, not the cost of the entire *project* itself, use of the separate-prime method may result in some categories of work being subject to formal bidding requirements while others may be subject to informal bidding requirements.

For example, a $750,000 construction project bid under the separate-prime method involves the following four categories of work with estimated costs for each of the four contracts:

1. HVAC	$125,000
2. Electrical	$75,000
3. Plumbing	$65,000
4. General	$485,000

Although the total cost of the project exceeds the formal bidding threshold of $500,000, the estimated cost of *each contract* falls within the informal bidding range, so the local government could use informal bidding procedures for each category of work. However, because the estimated cost of the *total project* exceeds $300,000, the additional requirements for large building projects discussed in this chapter apply (namely, that separate specifications must be drawn for the branches of work discussed in section V and formal HUB (historically underutilized business) participation requirements discussed in Chapter 4).

By comparison, taking the same $750,000 project described above and adjusting the estimated costs of each of the four contracts, a combination of formal and informal bidding requirements now apply.

1. HVAC	$75,000
2. Electrical	$75,000
3. Plumbing	$65,000
4. General	$535,000

Figure 3.3 Single-Prime Bidding Method

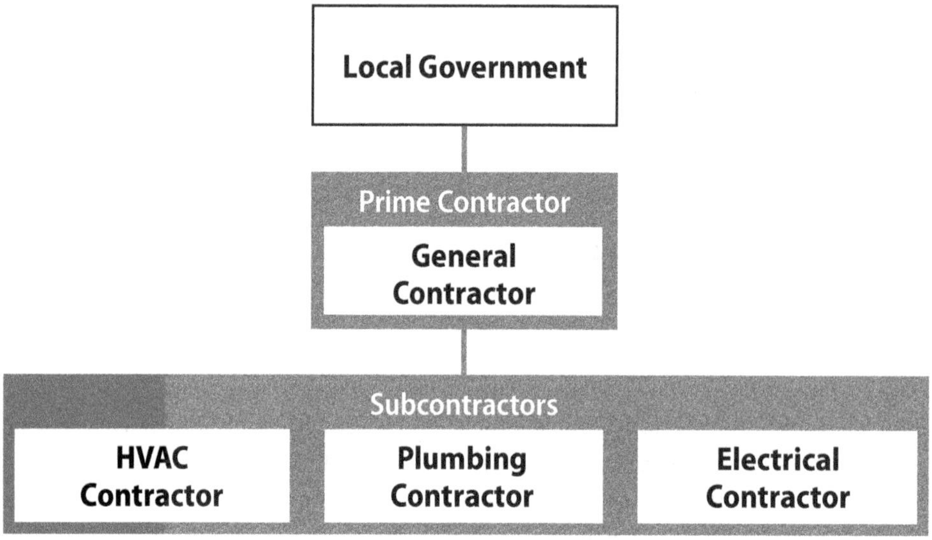

In this example, while the HVAC, electrical, and plumbing contracts remain within the informal bidding range, the general contract now falls into the formal bidding range, so the local government must use formal bidding procedures for the general contract—three bids must be received; bids must be sealed, in paper form, and submitted by the bid deadline; bids must be accompanied by a bid deposit of at least 5 percent of the bid amount; and bids must be opened in public. While the two different procedures may be used legally, for practical reasons a local government may in this instance choose to use formal bidding procedures for all contracts.

If some or all of the contracts on a project fall into the formal bidding range, it is possible that the first advertisement for proposals will elicit three or more bids for some of the branches of work and fewer than three bids for other branches. In that case, the board is free to award contracts for those branches for which the three-bid minimum rule is satisfied even though it must re-advertise the other branches for which the three-bid minimum was not satisfied (see section II.D.2 of Chapter 2 for a discussion of the three-bid minimum rule). If the board anticipates that rebidding for some branches may be necessary, it should specify that all bids submitted must be "firm" for a sufficient period of time (for example, forty-five to sixty days) in case it wants to delay its decision concerning award of any of the contracts until rebidding is completed.

B. Single-Prime Bidding

Local governments also have the option of soliciting bids for large building construction projects under the single-prime contracting system.[10] In single-prime contracting, contractors bid on performing all of the work required by the project for a specified price. The selected contractor hires and supervises the subcontractors used for various parts of the work.

The single-prime bidding method is illustrated in Figure 3.3. Under single-prime bidding, the governmental unit must use the same standard of award as for multiple-prime bidding. That is, it is to select the contractor that submits the lowest responsible, responsive bid for the project, taking into consideration quality, performance, and the time specified in the bids for the performance of the contract. However, under the single-prime system, the standard of award is applied to the award of just one contract, that being with the general contractor who is the only prime contractor on the project (meaning the local government contracts with only the general contractor).

Bidders under the single-prime approach must identify in their bids the subcontractors they intend to use for the four main subdivisions or branches of work for which separate specifications must be prepared—HVAC, electrical,

10. G.S. 143-128(d).

plumbing, and general. A contractor whose bid is accepted may substitute other subcontractors for those listed in the original bid only under one of the following three conditions:

1. the listed subcontractor's bid is later determined by the contractor to be nonresponsible or nonresponsive;
2. the listed subcontractor refuses to enter into a contract for the complete performance of the bid work; or
3. the awarding authority approves the substitution "for good cause shown by the contractor."

The terms, conditions, and requirements of each of the subcontracts must incorporate by reference the terms, conditions, and requirements of the contract between the contractor and the local government.

C. Dual-Bidding

A third contracting method authorized for large building construction projects is called dual-bidding.[11] The dual-bidding method is actually not a discrete contracting system but instead is a combination of separate-prime and single-prime bidding. Under the dual-bidding method, the local government solicits and accepts bids under both the single-prime and separate-prime contracting systems simultaneously. It then awards the contract to the lowest responsible, responsive bidder under either the single-prime system *or* the multiple-prime system. Moreover, it may make its award under one system *even if* the apparent lowest bidder's bid under the other system is lower. In either case, the local government is to take into consideration the other aspects of the usual award standard by considering quality, performance, and time specified in the bids to perform the contract. However, the public entity may also consider the cost of construction oversight, time for completion, and other factors it considers appropriate in determining under which system to award the contract.

Special requirements are imposed for submitting bids under the dual-bidding method. The deadline for submitting separate-prime bids must be at least one hour prior to the deadline for submitting single-prime bids. Both sets of bids are then opened at the single-prime deadline. In addition, the price that a subcontractor bids to a general contractor under the single-prime system cannot exceed the amount of its separate-prime bid, if any. These requirements are intended to prevent a subcontractor from quoting one price to a general contractor and then underbidding itself later in a separate-prime bid in an attempt to increase its chances of getting the work through the separate-prime system.

If the cost of the project falls into the formal bidding range ($500,000 or more), special rules apply to counting the number of bids received for purposes of complying with the three-bid minimum requirement (see section II.D.2 of Chapter 2 for further discussion of the three-bid minimum requirement). G.S. 143-132(b) specifies that a bid submitted by a single-prime contractor counts as one competitive bid for each of the four branches of work for which separate specifications must be drawn (HVAC, electrical, plumbing, and general) and that each full set of separate-prime bids constitutes a competitive single-prime bid. This means that the three-bid minimum rule is satisfied for projects bid under both the single-prime and separate-prime systems if any combination of single- and separate-prime bids is received that together "adds up to" three bids in each of the four categories of work (for example, one single-prime bid and two complete sets of separate-prime bids; three single-prime bids and no separate-prime bids; or three complete sets of separate-prime bids and no single-prime bids). However, if at least three single-prime bids have been received but not at least one full set of separate-prime bids, no separate-prime bids may be opened. In this case the governing board could, if it wished, open the single-prime bids and make an award from among them. It could also reject all of the bids and re-advertise.

Tables 3.2–3.7 demonstrate the various permutations on this rule and whether bids may be opened (an **X** indicating that a bid has been received). In the first example (Table 3.2), three bids (one complete set of separate-prime and two single-prime) have been received; all can be opened and the contract awarded in either category. In the second example (Table 3.3), two bids (no complete set of separate-prime and two single-prime) have been received; no bid can be opened, and the project must be re-advertised. In the third example (Table 3.4), three bids (no complete set of separate-prime and three single-prime) have been received; only single-prime bids can be

11. G.S. 143-128(d1).

Table 3.2 Three Bids Received: One Complete Set of Separate-Prime and Two Single-Prime

Separate-Prime (separate bids for each category)				Single-Prime (bid on all work)
HVAC	Electrical	Plumbing	General	
X	X	X	X	X
				X

Note: All bids can be opened, and a contract may be awarded in either category.

Table 3.3 Two Bids Received: No Complete Set of Separate-Prime and Two Single-Prime

Separate-Prime (separate bids for each category)				Single-Prime (bid on all work)
HVAC	Electrical	Plumbing	General	
X	X	X		X
				X

Note: No bids can be opened; project must be re-advertised.

Table 3.4 Three Bids Received: No Complete Set of Separate-Prime and Three Single-Prime

Separate-Prime (separate bids for each category)				Single-Prime (bid on all work)
HVAC	Electrical	Plumbing	General	
X	X	X		X
				X
				X

Note: Only single-prime bids can be opened; a contract may be awarded only in single-prime category, or the local government may choose to hold single-prime bids and re-advertise for separate-prime bids.

Table 3.5 Three Bids Received: No Complete Set of Separate-Prime and Three Single-Prime

Separate-Prime (separate bids for each category)				Single-Prime (bid on all work)
HVAC	Electrical	Plumbing	General	
X	X	X		X
X	X	X		X
	X			X

Note: Only single-prime bids can be opened, and a contract may be awarded only in single-prime category. Also note that bids in the electrical category cannot be opened even though three bids were received because no complete set of separate-prime bids were received.

Table 3.6 Two Bids Received: One Complete Set of Separate-Prime and One Single-Prime

Separate-Prime (separate bids for each category)				Single-Prime (bid on all work)
HVAC	Electrical	Plumbing	General	
X	X	X	X	X
X	X	X		
X		X		

Note: No bids can be opened, and the project must be re-advertised. Also note that bids in the HVAC and plumbing categories cannot be opened even though three bids were received in each category because a *total* of three bids were not received.

Table 3.7 Three Bids Received: Two Complete Sets of Separate-Prime and One Single-Prime

Separate-Prime (separate bids for each category)				Single-Prime (bid on all work)
HVAC	Electrical	Plumbing	General	
X	X	X	X	X
X	X	X	X	
X	X			

Note: All bids may be opened; contracts may be awarded in either category.

opened, and a contract may be awarded only in the single-prime category, or the local government may choose to hold the single-prime bids and re-advertise for separate-prime bids. In the fourth example (Table 3.5), three bids (no complete set of separate-prime and three single-prime) have been received; only the single-prime bids can be opened, and the contract may be awarded only in single-prime category. In the fifth example (Table 3.6), two bids (one complete set of separate-prime and one single-prime) have been received; no bids can opened, and the project must be re-advertised; also, bids in the HVAC and plumbing categories cannot be opened even though three bids were received in each category because a *total* of three bids were not received. In the sixth and final example (Table 3.7), three bids (two complete sets of separate-prime and one single-prime) were received; all bids may be opened and contracts awarded in either category.

VIII. Alternative Bidding and Construction Delivery Methods

A. Construction Management at-Risk

The construction management at-risk method adds an additional entity to the bidding and construction project, the construction manager at-risk (CMR).[12] The CMR is a construction manager who guarantees to the local government that he or she will construct the building to the architect's specifications for a guaranteed price. The CMR's profit and risk are built into the quoted price, which is "at-risk" for cost overruns on the project.

3.1. What is a CMR?

According to the definition in G.S. 143-128.1(a)(1), construction management services may include "preparation and coordination of bid packages, scheduling, cost control, value engineering, evaluation, preconstruction services, and construction administration." On a traditional construction project, use of construction managers is optional, and the actual tasks performed by particular construction managers vary. What the construction manager is to accomplish with respect to a specific project is set by contract.

A CMR, on the other hand, must meet specific requirements set by statute. The CMR must provide construction management services for the project throughout the preconstruction and construction phases, be licensed as a general contractor, and, as noted above, guarantee the cost of the project.[13] The CMR does not design the project under the North Carolina system; that work must be performed by a licensed architect or engineer working directly under contract with the local government.[14]

The CMR contracts directly with the public owner for all construction and acts as the public owner's fiduciary in handling and opening bids. Contractors performing construction work on the project contract directly with the CMR, not with the local government. The CMR also provides to the local government the performance and payment bonds required by G.S. Chapter 44A, Article 3, for contracts worth $50,000 or more on construction

12. G.S. 143-128.1.
13. G.S. 143-128.1(a)(2), -128.1(a)(3).
14. G.S. 143-128.1(b).

Figure 3.4 Construction Management at-Risk Contracting Method

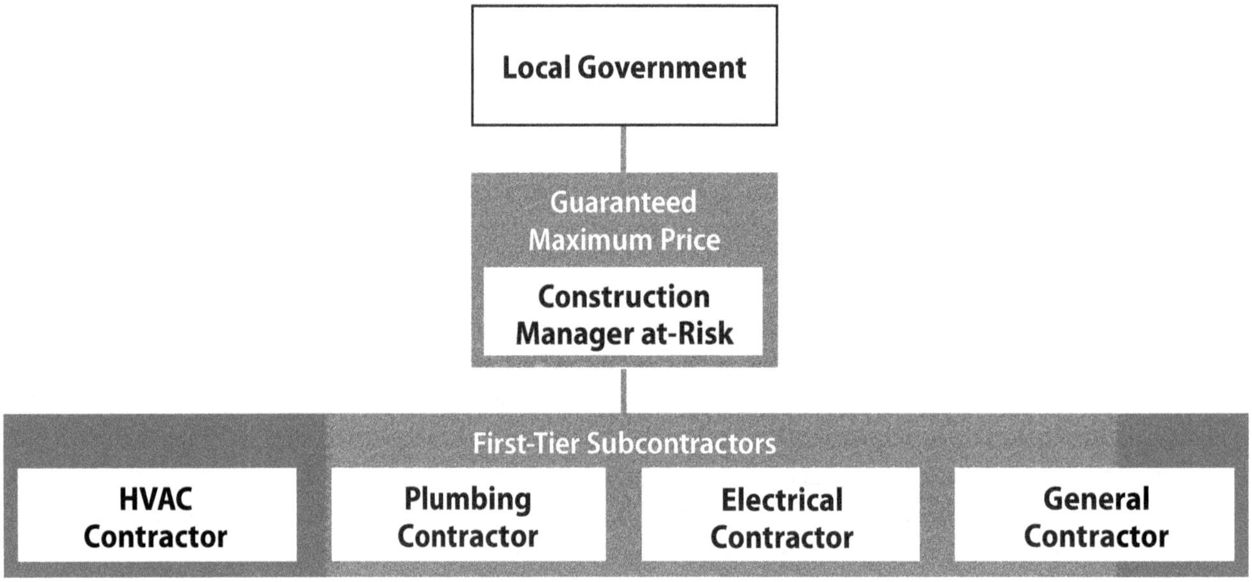

projects involving $300,000 or more. (See the discussion of performance and payment bonds in section II.H.2 of Chapter 2.)

The construction management at-risk contracting method is illustrated in Figure 3.4.

3.2. How is a CMR selected?

A CMR is selected using the same qualifications-based selection procedures as is required for hiring architects, engineers, and surveyors. These procedures are set out in G.S. Chapter 143, Article 3D, and discussed in Chapter 7. It is important to note here that, under the qualifications-based selection process, local governments are prohibited from soliciting fees during the request for qualifications (RFQ) process, and respondents are prohibited from submitting information on total estimated fees for the project. Fees can be negotiated only after the local government has evaluated the responses to the RFQ, ranked the respondents based on their qualifications and demonstrated competence to perform the work sought, and identified the best qualified firm. Only then can the local government negotiate fees and, initially, only with the best qualified firm. If the negotiations are not successful, the local government must terminate negotiations with the best qualified firm and initiate negotiations with the second-best qualified firm, and so on, until a firm is selected and a contract is awarded.

Prior to initiating the RFQ process for selecting a CMR, the local government must first make a determination that construction management at-risk services are in the best interest of the project.[15] The local government must also compare the advantages and disadvantages of using the CMR method in lieu of traditional construction bidding methods (single-prime, separate-prime, or dual-bidding). While governing board approval is not required by statute, the local government must perform this analysis itself and may not delegate this obligation to another entity (for example, to its architect or engineer). The CMR statute does not specifically require that the analysis be put in writing, but it is highly recommended that a local government do so.

3.3. When is the CMR's guaranteed price for the project established?

The CMR statute does not specify when the CMR's guaranteed price is to be set. One option is to negotiate and set the guaranteed maximum price before the CMR bids the actual construction work on the project. Another option is for the CMR and local government to agree to have the guaranteed maximum price determined *after* bids have

15. G.S. 143-128.1(e).

been received. If the latter procedure is used, the CMR obviously has a great deal more information concerning the project's likely cost at the time that it sets the guaranteed maximum price, and its extra fee for assuming the risk of an uncertain outcome should be lower. In addition, a local government may want to protect itself against excessive bid prices by including a clause in its contract with the CMR that allows it to terminate the CMR contract should the guaranteed price that is determined after bids are received exceeds the local government's budget for the project. In exercising this option, the local government would pay the CMR only for its expenses up to that point in time.

3.4. How does the CMR contract for the actual construction work?

The CMR conducts the bidding procedures for the construction work on behalf of the local government using any of the traditional bidding methods authorized by statute (single-prime, multiple-prime, or dual-bidding, all of which are discussed in section VII, above). The successful bidders do not contract directly with the local government; instead, they contract directly with the CMR who acts as the local government's fiduciary (meaning, the CMR "stands in the shoes" of the local government) in handling and opening bids. This places the obligation to comply with statutorily required competitive bidding requirements directly on the CMR. The bidders with which the CMR contracts are called first-tier subcontractors, and they are functionally equivalent to the separate-prime contractors on a multiple-prime construction project.

Regardless of whether the estimated costs of the construction contracts fall into the informal or formal bidding ranges, the CMR must publicly advertise for bids following the G.S. 143-129 requirements for formal bidding (see section II.B of Chapter 2 for further discussion of advertising requirements under formal bidding procedures). In addition, the CMR is required to prequalify all bidders for the various types of work required for the project using the prequalification procedures required under G.S. 143-135.8 (see section IV of Chapter 2 for a discussion of prequalification).[16] Only prequalified bidders may have their bids considered.

Because the CMR is required to use formal bidding procedures for advertising bids there must be a public bid opening, and once the bids are opened they become public records. The CMR, as the local government's fiduciary, is to award each contract according to the lowest responsive, responsible bidder standard, taking into consideration quality, performance, and the time specified in the bids for the performance of the contract. In addition, the CMR may consider the cost of construction oversight, the time for completion, and other factors deemed appropriate by the public entity and advertised as part of the bid solicitation. Note that the statute requires that the factors the local government has determined to be appropriate in considering contracts be included in the advertisement. In lieu of including a lengthy list of factors in the published ad, local governments may satisfy this requirement by listing those factors in the bid specifications and making reference to them in the bid advertisement.

The public entity may require the CMR to select a different first-tier subcontractor from the one the CMR prefers for any part of the work so long as the award standard set out above is followed and the CMR is compensated for any additional cost incurred.

3.5. How does the CMR prequalify bidders?

The CMR is required to prequalify all bidders on Tier 1 subcontracts using the prequalification procedures of G.S. 143-135.8 (see section IV of Chapter 2 for further discussion of prequalification). Consistent with the statutory prequalification procedures, the local government adopts a prequalification policy, and the CMR and the local government jointly develop the assessment tool and criteria for the specific project that the CMR is managing on behalf of the local government. The assessment tool and criteria must include the prequalification scoring values and the minimum required score required for bidders to achieve prequalification on that project.

3.6. Do HUB requirements apply to a project constructed under the CMR method?

Yes. The CMR must submit to the local government for approval its plan for complying with the HUB participation requirements of G.S. 143-128.2 prior to soliciting bids for the project's first-tier subcontractors. Both the CMR and

---

16. G.S. 143-128.1(c).

these subcontractors must make a good faith effort to recruit and select minority businesses for participation in contracts, in accordance with that statute's provisions (see Chapter 4 for further discussion of HUB requirements).

3.7. Since the CMR must be a licensed general contractor, can the CMR perform any of the construction work?

The CMR is not permitted to perform any of the construction work that is part of the project except in limited circumstances authorized under the CMR statute. The CMR may perform construction work on the project only with the local government's approval in three particular situations: (1) if the bidding process produces no responsible, responsive bidder for that part of the work, (2) if the selected bidder refuses to execute a contract for the bid portion of the work, or (3) if the selected subcontractor defaults and a prequalified replacement cannot be obtained in a timely manner.

B. Design-Build

Until 2013, local governments were able to utilize the design-build construction delivery method only with the approval of the State Building Commission or the General Assembly by local act. Now, design-build is statutorily authorized for all public entities in North Carolina, including local governments.[17]

3.8. What is design-build?

The design-build method is an integrated approach that delivers both design (architectural and engineering) and construction services under one contract with a single point of responsibility. Under design-build, the public owner is provided the benefit of the design team and contractor working together to achieve the public owner's objectives under a single contract. The designer works directly with the contractor instead of for the public owner.[18]

Design-build is sometimes confused with CMR, which has been authorized under G.S. 143-128 for over a decade.[19] One fundamental difference between design-build and CMR is that, under CMR, the local government is required to contract separately with an architect and/or engineer for design services, whereas a design-build project involves a single contract with both the design professional and the contractor encompassing the design *and* construction phases of the project. Under CMR, the designer works directly for the public owner; under design-build, the designer works with the contractor.

Under design-build, project specifications are not drawn prior to initiating the contracting process. Instead, the public owner advertises general information about the project and selects the design-builder based on its qualifications to design and construct the project. Once under contract, the design-builder (a team comprising the designer and the general contractor) works with the owner to design the project based on the owner's project criteria, usually by preparing a preliminary design followed by detailed specifications after the owner's approval of the preliminary design. The design work can be done in phases, allowing construction to commence and proceed in phases to expedite project completion, or the design work can be finalized prior to construction. Under either system, the designer continues to work with the builder throughout the project in addressing unforeseen issues or design revisions as the project proceeds.

3.9. Who is a design-builder (or design-build team)?

The design-build statute defines a design-builder as "an appropriately licensed person, corporation, or entity that, under a single contract, offers to provide or provides design services and general contracting services."[20] Architectural and engineering services must be performed by licensed architects and engineers, and contractor services must be performed by a licensed general contractor. While it is possible for one individual to hold both an engineering license and a general contractor license, a design-builder typically is a corporation, firm, or joint venture

17. G.S. 143-128.1A (S.L. 2013-401).

18. N.C. State Building Commission, Resolution on Design/Build Construction (adopted May 22, 2012), www.nc-sco.com/documents/sbc/SBCDesignBuildResolutions8-28-12.pdf.

19. Construction management at-risk was statutorily authorized by the General Assembly for all public agencies in 2001. S.L. 2001-496, sects. 2, 3.

20. G.S. 143-128.1A(a)(1), cross-referencing -128.1B(a)(2).

that employs both licensed design professionals and licensed general contractors, or, a construction firm that subcontracts with an architect or engineer. The new design-build statute requires the design-builder to certify that each licensed designer and subconsultant who is a member of the design-build team was selected based on "demonstrated competence and qualifications" under the qualifications-based selection process of the Mini-Brooks Act (see Chapter 7 for a full discussion of the Mini-Brooks Act).[21]

3.10. What is the process for entering into a design-build contract?

To enter into a design-build contract, the unit of government must follow specific procurement procedures set out in G.S. 143-128.1A. Under the design-build contracting process, the local government must

1. adopt written criteria for using the design-build method,
2. give public notice of and issue an RFQ,
3. include specific information in the RFQ,
4. receive and evaluate responses to the RFQ (a three-response minimum is required to consider proposals),
5. require the selected design-builder to furnish performance and payment bonds.

In addition, the statute places limits on when a design-builder, once under contract, may substitute key personnel identified in the design-builder's response to the local government's RFQ.

3.11. What criteria must be adopted?

To initiate the design-build contracting process, the local government must establish written criteria for determining when design-build is appropriate for a project.[22] While the criteria must be in writing, governing board approval is not specifically required (though highly advisable). The statute requires the local government to adopt the criteria for *each* project. These criteria must address at least the following six factors:

1. the local government's ability to "adequately and thoroughly" define the project requirements in the RFP;
2. time constraints for project delivery;
3. the local government's ability to ensure that a quality project can be delivered;
4. the availability of qualified staff or outside consultants experienced in design-build to manage and oversee the project;
5. good faith efforts to comply with HUB participation requirements (G.S. 143-128.2 and -128.4) and to recruit and select small business entities (the term "small business entities" is not defined in the statute); and
6. the criteria used by the local government, including a comparison of the advantages and disadvantages of using design-build in lieu of traditional construction bidding methods.

3.12. What kind of public notice is required?

After adopting its criteria, the local government must issue a public notice of an RFQ for the project.[23] Note that the notice must be made public but is not required to be *published.* The statute does not specify a minimum time for or method of notice (for example, formal published notice in a newspaper for seven days is not required). Since a design-builder is selected under the qualifications-based selection method of the Mini-Brooks Act, units may wish to use the same notice procedures they employ for announcing requirements for architects and engineers. In the alternative, units could choose to follow the published notice procedures for formal purchase and construction contracts under G.S. 143-129(b). As with other contracts subject to the Mini-Brooks Act, the unit must make good faith efforts to notify minority firms of the opportunity to submit qualifications.[24]

---

21. G.S. 143-128.1A(e).
22. G.S. 143-128.1A(b).
23. G.S. 143-128.1A(c).
24. G.S. 143-64.31(a).

3.13. What must be included in the RFQ?

The RFQ issued by the local government must include information on the following eight items:[25]

1. project site;
2. project scope;
3. anticipated project budget;
4. project schedule;
5. qualifications selection criteria and criteria weighting;
6. notice of the local government's rules, ordinances, or goals (presumably related to the project), including goals for HUB and small business participation (the statute does not define "small business"; some local governments have small business participation programs authorized by the General Assembly through a local act);
7. other information provided by the local government to potential design-bidders in submitting qualifications for the project; and
8. a statement requiring each design-builders to submit *with* its response to the RFQ an explanation of its project team selection consisting of either
    a. a list of licensed contractors, licensed subcontractors, and licensed design professionals the design-builder proposes to use on the project or
    b. the design-builder's strategy for selecting contractors and subcontractors based on the requirements of Article 8 of Chapter 143 (in other words, competitive bidding procedures).

Note: Design-builders must also certify that each licensed design professional who is a member of the design-build team, including subconsultants, was selected through the qualifications-based selection method required under the Mini-Brooks Act.[26] While it appears that this certification is required of each design-builder submitting a proposal in response to the local government's RFQ, it is unclear whether the certification must be submitted with the proposal, as is the case with the project team members or selection strategy described above. Local governments can clarify this uncertainty by specifically stating in the RFQ that the certification be submitted with the proposal.

3.14. Must a minimum number of proposals be received?

In order to consider proposals, the local government must receive at least three responses to its RFQ.[27] If the unit receives less than three responses, it must re-solicit (this requirement mirrors the "three-bid minimum" rule for formal construction bids[28]). After the second solicitation, the local government may consider proposals even if three are not received. As with the initial solicitation, the statute does not specify a method or time frame for re-solicitation, so local governments should follow the same procedures used for the initial solicitation.

3.15. Must proposals be submitted sealed and opened at a public bid opening?

The design-build statute does not require either that proposals be submitted sealed or that they be opened at a public bid opening. The local government is free to do either or both if it chooses. If proposals are not required to be submitted sealed, the proposals are subject to public inspection when the local government receives them. If they are required to be submitted sealed, the proposals become open to public inspection once they are unsealed.

3.16. How are proposals evaluated and the contract awarded?

After receiving proposals, the local government evaluates them and ranks the three most qualified respondents based on the criteria included in the RFQ.[29] The unit then negotiates a contract at a "fair and reasonable price" with the highest ranked design-builder. As with other contracts subject to the Mini-Brooks Act, the unit cannot

---

25. G.S. 143-128.1A(c).
26. G.S. 143-128.1A(e).
27. G.S. 143-128.1A(d).
28. G.S. 143-132.
29. G.S. 143-128.1A(d), (e); -64.31.

Figure 3.5 The Design-Build Construction Delivery Method

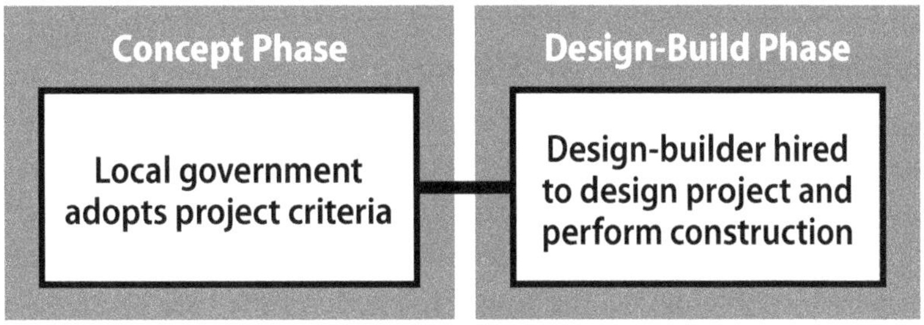

Figure 3.6 The Design-Build Bridging Construction Delivery Method

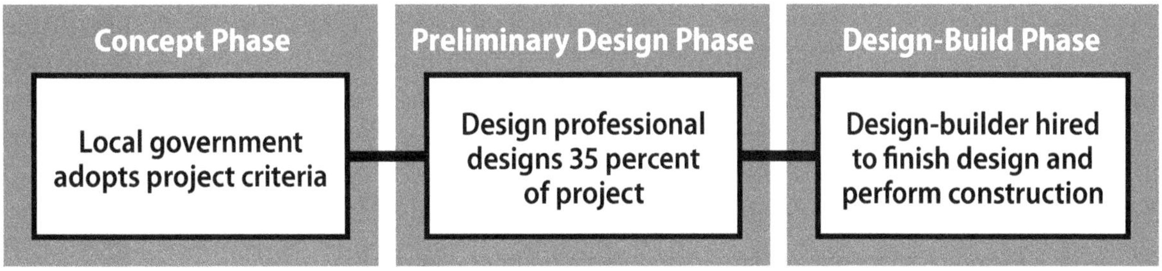

solicit project cost estimates or fees in the RFQ and can only negotiate contract price after ranking the respondents based on qualifications. If negotiations with the highest ranked respondent are not successful, the local government may initiate negotiations with the second highest ranked respondent and so on, until the local government either rejects all proposals or selects a design-builder with whom to contract. During its evaluation process, the local government may, if it so chooses, interview some or all of the respondents. The design-build statute does not require governing board approval of the contract award, even for projects costing $500,000 or more (which, under traditional construction bidding methods, do require governing board approval).

3.17. What are the bond requirements?

Once the contract award decision is made, the selected design-builder must provide bonds under Article 3 of Chapter 44A, which requires performance and payment bonds for 100 percent of the contract amount for each contract costing more than $50,000 on projects costing over $300,000 (see Section II.H.2 of Chapter 2 for discussion of performance and payment bonds).[30]

3.18. What are the limitations on substituting key personnel?

Once the contract has been awarded, the design-builder can substitute key personnel (the contractors, subcontractors, and design professionals identified in the design-builder's response to the RFQ) only after obtaining written approval from the local government.[31] This requirement does not apply if the design-builder selects contractors and subcontractors under the competitive bidding requirements of Article 8 of Chapter 143. Since design professionals are not selected under Article 8 but instead are selected using the qualifications-based selection process under the Mini-Brooks Act, it is unclear whether this exception applies to substituting design professionals. Local governments could address this ambiguity in the terms and conditions of the contract with the design-builder.

---

30. G.S. 143-128.1A(f); G.S. 44A-26.
31. G.S. 143-128.1A(f).

C. Design-Build Bridging

Design-build bridging is another alternative construction delivery method authorized by the General Assembly in 2013.[32] While similar in concept to design-build, it differs in several significant ways.

3.19. What is design-build bridging, and how is it different from design-build?

The design-build bridging construction method is a two-step contracting and construction delivery process that differs from design-build in two significant ways. First, the local government contracts separately with an architect or engineer to design 35 percent of the project (referred to in the statute as the "design criteria"[33]). The local government then solicits proposals from design-build firms based on the design criteria package and contracts with a design-builder to complete the remainder of the design and perform the construction work. The design criteria act as "bridging" documents between initial project concept and the design-build phase—hence the name of this construction method. These bridging documents provide enough project requirements in preliminary drawings and specifications to enable design-build bidders to submit a responsive bid.[34]

The second difference between design-build bridging and design-build involves the solicitation of fees and the standard of award for the contract. Under the design-build method, fees cannot be solicited in the RFQ for design-build services and the contract is awarded based on the qualifications-based selection method of the Mini-Brooks Act (see Chapter 7 for a full discussion of the Mini-Brooks Act). Under the design-build bridging method, however, fees and price estimates *are* solicited in the RFP for design-build services and the contract for these services is awarded based on the lowest responsive, responsible bidder standard.

The design-build method is illustrated in Figure 3.5; the design-build bridging method, in Figure 3.6.

3.20. What is the process for entering into a design-build bridging contract?

To enter into a design-build bridging contract the local government must follow specific procedures set out in G.S. 143-128.1B. While many aspects of these procedures mirror those for design-build (see section VIII.B, immediately above), there are some notable differences. Local governments should be aware of these differences and take them into account when considering whether design-build or design-build bridging is an appropriate construction delivery method for a particular project.

Under the design-build bridging contracting process the local government must

1. adopt written criteria for using the design-build bridging method;
2. issue an RFQ and select a preliminary design professional using the qualifications-based selection process under the Mini-Brooks Act (the preliminary design professional then develops the design criteria package for use in selecting a design-builder);
3. issue an RFP based on the design criteria package to solicit proposals from design-builders;
4. receive and evaluate responses to the RFP (a three-response minimum is required to consider proposals);
5. require the selected design-builder to furnish performance and payment bonds.

3.21. Must the local government adopt criteria, and if so, what are they?

To initiate the design-build bridging contracting process, the local government must establish written criteria for determining when using this method is appropriate for a project.[35] The criteria must be in writing, but governing board approval is not specifically required. The statute does require the local government to adopt the criteria for each project (in other words, it cannot adopt blanket criteria). The criteria must address the same six factors as required for a design-build project:

---

32. G.S. 143-128.1B (S.L. 2013-401).

33. G.S. 143-128.1B(a)(3).

34. *Id.* Because of the cost involved in preparing a response to a design-build solicitation, the North Carolina State Building Commission recommends that local governments develop bridging documents to reduce costs to potential bidders and encourage competition.

35. G.S. 143-128.1B(b).

1. the local government's ability to "adequately and thoroughly" define the project requirements in the RFP;
2. time constraints for project delivery;
3. the local government's ability to ensure that a quality project can be delivered;
4. the availability of qualified staff or outside consultants experienced in design-build to manage and oversee the project;
5. good faith efforts to comply with HUB participation requirements (G.S. 143-128.2 and -128.4) and to recruit and select small business entities (the term "small business entities" is not defined in the statute); and
6. the criteria used by the local government, including a comparison of the advantages and disadvantages of using design-build bridging in lieu of traditional construction bidding methods.

3.22. How is the preliminary design professional selected?

Before issuing the RFP for design-build services, a local government first either selects a staff design professional (an architect or engineer employed by the local government) or follows the Mini-Brooks Act to contract with an architect or engineer. This design professional (whether it be an employee or an outside design professional) develops the design criteria package and acts as the local government's representative during the design-build contracting process and throughout the life of the project. The design professional is not eligible to bid on the design-build contract or provide input to a design-build bidder during the bidding process.

3.23. What must be included in the design criteria package?

The preliminary design professional develops the design criteria for the project in consultation with the local government and prepares a design package consisting of 35 percent of the design documentation for the entire project.[36] This design criteria package forms the basis upon which proposals from design-builders are solicited. The design criteria package must include the following nine items:

1. programmatic needs, interior space requirements, intended space utilization, and other capacity requirements;
2. physical characteristics of the site, such as a topographic survey;
3. material quality standards or performance criteria;
4. special material requirements;
5. provisions for utilities;
6. parking requirements;
7. type, size, and location of adjacent structures;
8. preliminary or conceptual drawings and specifications in sufficient detail to enable design-build teams to submit responsive bids; and
9. notice of the local government's rules, ordinances, or goals (presumably related to the project).

3.24. What kind of public notice is required?

After developing the design criteria package, the local government must issue a public notice of an RFP for design-build firms to complete the design and perform the construction.[37] As with the design-build method, the statute does not specify the minimum time for or method of publication. Since the design-build contract under this method is awarded based on the lowest responsive, responsible bidder standard of award (discussed in question 3.28, below), local governments may wish to follow the published notice procedures for formal bidding under G.S. 143-129(b).

36. G.S. 143-128.1B(c).
37. G.S. 143-128.1B(d).

3.25. What must be included in the RFP?

The RFP must include general information on the same eight items required for a design-build RFQ but must also include the following two additional elements:[38]

1. the design criteria package prepared by the preliminary design professional and
2. a statement that each design-build bidder must submit *with its proposal in a sealed envelope* its price for providing the general conditions of the contract and fees for design services and general construction services.

The solicitation of fees and prices is a significant departure from the design-build process, which prohibits soliciting fee and price estimates in the RFQ for design-build services. Note also that this information must be submitted with the bidder's proposal in a separate sealed envelope; a bid that does not contain sealed fee and price proposals would be considered nonresponsive. In addition, each bidder must certify that all members of its design-build team who are licensed design professionals, including subconsultants, were selected as required under the Mini-Brooks Act.

3.26. Must a minimum number of proposals be received?

As with design-build, the local government must receive at least three responses to its RFP in order to consider proposals.[39] If the local government receives less than three responses, it must re-solicit (just as is required for formal construction bids). After the second advertisement, the local government may consider proposals even if three are not received.

3.27. Must proposals be submitted sealed and opened at a public bid opening?

As with design-build, the design-build bridging statute does not require either that proposals be submitted sealed or that they be opened at a public bid opening. The local government is free to do either or both if it chooses. If proposals are not required to be submitted sealed, the proposals are subject to public inspection when the local government receives them. If they are required to be submitted sealed, the proposals become open to public inspection once they are unsealed.

3.28. How are proposals evaluated and the contract awarded?

After receiving proposals, the local government evaluates and ranks them and then groups the top three without specific ordinal ranking (meaning it identifies the top three proposals but does not put them in specific priority order).[40] From among these three respondents the unit selects the design-builder who is the lowest responsive, responsible bidder based on the cumulative amount of fees for providing the general conditions of the contract, design services, and general construction services taking into consideration quality, performance, and the time specified in the proposal for performance of the contract. This standard of award is substantially different from that for design-build where the design-builder is selected based on qualifications.

3.29. What are the bond requirements?

As with design-build, the selected design-builder must provide bonds under Article 3 of Chapter 44A, which requires performance and payment bonds for 100 percent of the contract amount for each contract costing more than $50,000 on projects costing over $300,000 (see section II.H.2 of Chapter 2 for a discussion of these bonds).[41]

3.30. What are the limitations on substituting key personnel and hiring subcontractors?

Once the contract is awarded, the winning design-builder can substitute key personnel only after obtaining written approval from the unit of government.[42] In addition, the design-builder with whom the unit contracts must use

---

38. *Id.*
39. G.S. 143-128.1B(e).
40. *Id.*
41. G.S. 143-128.1B(f).
42. G.S. 143-128.1B(g).

the competitive bidding requirements of Article 8 of Chapter 143 in hiring first-tier subcontractors on the project (design professionals are not considered first-tier subcontractors).[43]

D. Public-Private Partnerships

The basic concept of the public-private partnership method (P3) is to provide flexible contracting authority under which local governments can partner with a private developer for the construction, operation, and financing of a capital project. As with design-build and design-build bridging, P3's have been statutorily authorized for all public entities since 2013.[44]

3.31. What is a public-private partnership?

A public-private project is defined under G.S. 143-128.1C as a "capital improvement project undertaken for the benefit of a governmental entity and private developer pursuant to a development contract that includes construction of a public facility or other improvements, including paving, grading, utilities, infrastructure, reconstruction, or repair, and may include both public and private facilities."[45] Under the P3 construction delivery method, the unit of government is authorized to acquire, construct, own, lease (as lessor or lessee), and operate a public-private project or facilities within a public-private project and may make loans or grants for these purposes. Important to note is that the private developer must provide at least 50 percent of the financing for the total cost of the project.[46] The Local Government Commission must approve the contract if it involves a capital or operating lease.[47]

3.32. What is the process for entering into a P3 contract?

To enter into a P3 contract, units of government must comply with the statutory requirements set out in G.S. 143-128.1C. The procedures are similar to those required for design-build and design-build bridging contracts only in that they are based on the Mini-Brooks Act. Otherwise, the P3 procurement requirements are substantially different.

Under the P3 contracting method the local government must

1. make written findings that it has a critical need for the project,
2. determine its programming needs for the project,
3. publish a formal notice of an RFQ to solicit proposals from interested developers (specific information must be included in the RFQ and solicited from potential respondents),
4. receive and evaluate responses to the RFQ,
5. comply with specific procedures for awarding the contract,
6. address specific factors in the development contract.

---

43. G.S. 143-128.1B(f), -128.1B(a)(5).

44. Public-private partnerships are not new in North Carolina. This type of contracting method has been authorized from time to time by the General Assembly, such as for the Department of Revenue's Tax Information Management System in 2009 (S.L. 2009-451, sec. 6.20), the Town of Matthews in 2010 (S.L. 2010-52), Onslow County in 2013 (S.L. 2013-37), and certain N.C. Department of Transportation projects (G.S. 136-28.1) and toll roads (S.L. 2012-184). Similar public-private financing authorization has been available for well over a decade for NCSU's Centennial Campus, UNC-CH's Horace Williams Campus, and the Millennial Campuses of other UNC constituent institutions (Article 21B of Chapter 116). Public schools have had public-private partnership authorization for built-to-suit capital leases since 2006 (G.S. 115C-532; this statute expires July 1, 2015). And, since 1987, cities have been able to undertake public-private partnerships as part of a downtown development project, though that statute's authority is geographically limited to capital projects in a city's central business district (CBD) (G.S. 160A-458.3). Public-private partnerships were the subject of a 2009 legislative study commission and a study by NCSU's Institute for Emerging Issues. What is new since 2013 is the statutory framework of G.S. 143-128.1C and the availability of this contracting and financing method for any unit of local government without having to obtain specific legislative authorization through a local act.

45. G.S. 143-128.1C(a)(8).

46. G.S. 143-128.1C(b).

47. G.S. 143-128.1C(j). A capital or operating lease involving a public school cannot contain provisions relating to student assignment (G.S. 143-128.1C(l)).

3.33. What written findings must be adopted?

To initiate the P3 contracting process, a unit of government must make findings in writing that it has a critical need for the project. While the statute does not specifically require governing board approval, entities categorized as a public body under the Open Meetings Act (Article 33C of Chapter 143) must make these findings at an open meeting of the body, which for local governments means the governing board must approve the findings. Unlike the design-build and design-build bridging statutes, there are no specific criteria that must be adopted by the governing board other than a finding that there is a critical need for the project.

3.34. How does the local government determine its programming needs?

After the governing board's approval of using the P3 method, the local government must determine its programming requirements for the facilities to be constructed under the P3 contract and the form in which private developers are to submit their qualifications. This information forms the basis of the RFQ the unit advertises. The P3 statute does not specify what or how the programming needs are to be determined, so a local government is free to identify whatever programming needs for the facility it deems are in its best interest (for example, the amount of parking and office space needed, information technology requirements, whether conference rooms or public gathering spaces are needed, etc.).

3.35. How does the local government advertise the RFQ?

The unit must advertise notice for interested private developers to submit their qualifications. The advertisement must be published in a newspaper of general circulation within the county in which the unit is located. The statute does not specify a minimum time frame for the publication period, but units should choose a time sufficient for interested parties to develop a proposal taking into consideration the complexity of a P3 project. While the unit is not required to publish the programming requirements in the advertisement itself, it must make these requirements available to potential respondents in whatever form the unit deems appropriate.[48]

3.36. What are the requirements for receiving responses? Is a minimum number of responses required, and must the responses be submitted sealed and opened in public?

The local government may choose to receive responses to its RFQ in any form it deems appropriate. Sealed proposals and a public opening are not required. Unlike the design-build and design-build bridging methods, a minimum number of responses is not required, so a local government may evaluate and award a contract even if only one response is received.

3.37. What information must developers submit in their responses to the RFQ?

Private developers must submit the following information as part of their response to the RFQ:[49]

1. evidence of financial stability (the statute specifies that information that constitutes a "trade secret" under G.S. 66-152(3) remains confidential);
2. experience with similar projects;
3. an explanation of project team selection by either listing licensed contractors, licensed subcontractors, and licensed design professionals whom the private developer proposes to use for the project's design and construction or outlining in a statement a strategy for open contractor and subcontractor selection based on competitive bidding procedures;
4. a statement of the developer's availability to undertake the public-private project and projected time line for completion;
5. any other information required by the governmental entity.

---

48. G.S. 143-128.1C(h).
49. *Id.*

3.38. How are proposals evaluated?

The local government may award the development contract to the private developer it determines to be best qualified, which is the standard of award under the Mini-Brooks Act (see Chapter 7 for a full discussion of the Mini-Brooks Act). However, unlike in a traditional Mini-Brooks Act selection process, the unit is not required to rank proposals based on qualifications and may negotiate with one or more of the respondents during the evaluation process. The statute is silent on the criteria the local government must use in evaluating the qualifications of the respondents, so it is free to develop its own criteria based on its programming needs, project scope, and any other factors related to the project it deems appropriate.

3.39. What are the requirements for awarding the contract?

A P3 contract must be awarded by the local government's governing board at an open meeting after a public hearing and at least thirty days' published notice of the public hearing and the terms of the contract (this last requirement necessitates negotiating all the terms and conditions of the contract prior to governing board approval). The terms of the contract and the public hearing must be included in the same advertisement, which must be published in a newspaper of general circulation within the county in which the unit is located. The unit also must make available a summary of the contract terms and conditions and indicate how to obtain a copy of the complete contract.[50] Only after thirty days of published notice and a public hearing can the governing board approve the P3 contract.

3.40. What must be included in the P3 contract?

The development contract between the local government and the private developer specifies the parties' interests, roles, and responsibilities.[51] At a minimum, the contract must address

1. the property interests of the local government and the private developer (this could include both ownership and lease arrangements),
2. the development responsibilities of the local government and the private developer (this could include both construction and ongoing operation and maintenance activities),
3. the financing responsibilities of the local government and the private developer (remember that the private developer must finance at least 50 percent of the total cost of the project),
4. the parties' good faith efforts to comply with HUB participation requirements and to recruit and select small business entities (the term "small business entities" is not defined in the statute).

Under the development contract, the local government may require the developer to be responsible for some or all of the construction, the purchase of materials and equipment, compliance with HUB participation requirements and to use the same contractor(s) as the local government (assuming all the contracting is not handled by the private developer). It also may require the developer to purchase materials for the project at a reasonable price. If the project utilizes the design-build construction delivery method, the contracting requirements of the design-build statute (G.S. 143-128.1A) must be followed.

3.41. What are the bond requirements?

The P3 statute requires the developer to provide payment bonds of 100 percent of the total anticipated amount of the construction contracts to be entered into between the private developer and the contractors the developer employs to design or construct the project as required by the development contract. The statute sets out specific procedures for claims under a payment bond made against the private developer.[52] Note that this payment bond requirement differs from that of G.S. Chapter 44A, Article 3, for traditional construction projects.

50. G.S. 143-128.1C(i).
51. G.S. 143-128.1C(b).
52. G.S. 143-128.1C(g).

The P3 statute does not require the developer to provide a performance bond to the local government. However, the statute authorizes the local government to require one if it so chooses.[53]

3.42. Can the private developer perform any of the design or construction work?

The private developer with whom the local government contracts cannot perform any design or construction work on the project unless a contractor defaults or a qualified replacement cannot be obtained in a timely manner and the local government approves.[54]

3.43. Do HUB requirements apply to P3 projects?

The private developer and its contractors must comply with state HUB participation requirements, which include bidders' good faith efforts to solicit historically underutilized businesses on building construction projects costing $300,000 or more. In addition, if the local government contracts for any of the construction work on the project it too is subject to state HUB requirements (see Chapter 4 for a full discussion of HUB requirements).

E. Other Alternative Contracting Methods

The State Building Commission may authorize local governments and other entities subject to G.S. 143-129 (the formal bidding statutes) to use other methods of construction contracting besides those authorized under G.S. 143-128.[55] This authorization, if granted, applies only to a single project and requires approval by a majority of the members of the commission present and voting.[56] The commission may authorize a project if the local government demonstrates that the alternative contracting method is necessary because the project cannot be reasonably completed under the methods authorized in G.S. 143-128. The commission also may authorize the alternative method under a "catch-all" provision that allows it to approve projects for other reasons that the commission deems appropriate and in the public's interest, pursuant to its rules and criteria.[57] In granting the authorization, the commission may not waive the requirements of G.S. 143-129 (formal bidding) or -132 (the "three-bid" rule discussed in section II.D.2 of Chapter 2) unless otherwise authorized by law. If the authorization is granted, the local government must include in its bid proposal for the project a requirement that the contractor file a plan for making a good faith effort to reach the minority participation goal set out in G.S. 143-128.2.

F. Reporting Requirements

Under G.S. 143-133.1, when a local government uses any of the statutorily authorized alternative delivery methods discussed above—construction management at-risk, design-build, design-build bridging, or public-private partnership—it is to report certain information to the North Carolina Secretary of Administration through the Department of Administration's Office of Historically Underutilized Businesses.

The information includes

a. a detailed explanation of the reason why the particular construction manager at-risk, design-builder, or private developer was selected;
b. the terms of the contract;
c. a list of all other firms considered but not selected;
d. a report on the form of bidding utilized by the construction manager at-risk, design-builder, or private developer on the project;

---

53. G.S. 143-128.1C(g)(1).
54. G.S. 143-128.1C(f).
55. G.S. 143-128(a1)(5).
56. G.S. 143-135.26(9).
57. The commission's rules for dealing with alternative construction method projects may be found in N.C. ADMIN. CODE tit. 1, ch. 30G, §§ .0101–0105.

e. a detailed explanation of why the particular alternative construction delivery method was used in lieu of a traditional delivery method (single-prime, separate-prime, or dual-bidding) and the anticipated benefits from using the particular construction delivery method.[58]

The report required by this statute must be submitted no later than twelve months from the date the local government takes beneficial occupancy of the project. Failure to do so results in the inability of the local government to use an alternative construction delivery method until the report is filed. However, a contract entered into in violation of this requirement remains valid and enforceable. A contractor or firm who submitted a bid or proposal on any project previously advertised by the local government is entitled to obtain an injunction against the local government compelling it to comply with the reporting requirements; however, the bidder who files such an action is not entitled to recover monetary damages or attorneys' fees. The action must be filed within four years from the date on which the local government took beneficial occupancy of the project for which the report is due.[59]

IX. Other Building Construction Requirements

A. Acting as Your Own General Contractor—The Owner-Contractor Affidavit Requirement

3.44. When can a local government act as its own general contractor?

G.S. 87-1 requires any construction or repair project costing $30,000 or more to be superintended (supervised) by a general contractor licensed in this state. Exempt from this requirement are *building* construction projects where the property owner, including local governments, intends to solely occupy the building being altered or built *on its own property.* If the building is not occupied solely by the property owner for at least twelve months following completion of the project, it is presumed that the property owner did not intend to solely occupy the building.[60] If eligible for the owner-contractor exemption, the property owner can, in essence, act as its own general contractor and perform the duty of superintending the project itself. However, the property owner cannot obtain a building permit under this exemption and then delegate this duty to an unlicensed person. This duty can be delegated only to a licensed general contractor.

If a local government wishes to use its own employees instead of hiring a general contractor to undertake any construction or repair project costing $30,000 or more, the project must qualify under the force account exception of G.S. 143-135, which is discussed in detail in section II of Chapter 5. In addition, if that project involves a *building,* the local government is required to submit an affidavit to the local building inspector verifying its eligibility for the owner-contractor exemption (this requirement applies also to private property owners).[61]

3.45. What is the owner-contractor affidavit, and what must it contain?

The owner-contractor affidavit is the legal document (an affidavit is a sworn, written statement attesting to the truth of the contents of the statement) verifying the property owner's eligibility for the owner-contractor exemption to general contractor licensure requirements. The person executing the affidavit on behalf of the local government must attest to three facts, as follows:

1. the person is the owner of the property on which the building is being constructed or altered, or, if the property is owned by a firm or corporation or local government, the person is legally authorized to act on that entity's behalf;
2. the person will personally superintend and manage all aspects of the construction or alteration of the building and will not delegate this duty to any other person who is not a licensed general contractor; and

58. G.S. 143-133.1(a).
59. G.S. 143-133.1(c).
60. G.S. 87-1(b)(2).
61. G.S. 87-14(a)(1).

3. the person will be personally present for all building inspections required under the North Carolina State Building Code (this last requirement does not apply if the plans for the building were drawn and sealed by a licensed architect).

The local building inspector must receive the affidavit prior to issuing a building permit. Although not required to do so, a local building inspector may ask questions, require the property owner to fill out a questionnaire or form, or request additional information in determining whether the property owner appears to qualify for the exemption prior to issuing the building permit.

Once the local building inspector receives the affidavit, he is required to submit the affidavit to the North Carolina Licensing Board for General Contractors for verification that the property owner is eligible under the owner-contractor exemption. If the board determines that the property owner is *not* eligible for the exemption, the building permit issued for the construction project *must* be revoked.[62] In addition, local building inspectors are prohibited from conducting building inspections during construction if the property owner is not personally present during the inspection (this prohibition does not apply if the building plans were drawn and sealed by a licensed architect).

3.46. Who may execute an owner-contractor affidavit on behalf of a local government?

G.S. 87-14(a)(1) does not specify which employee or official is authorized to execute and submit the affidavit on behalf of the local government. Given the formal requirement of submitting a verified affidavit, the individual should be

1. legally authorized to act on behalf of the unit of government (such as the manager, finance officer, or public works director);
2. capable of personally supervising the construction project (the individual does not have to be a licensed general contractor but should be someone with enough knowledge and experience to properly supervise the construction project);
3. able to be personally present at all building inspections (unless the plans are drawn and sealed by a licensed architect); and
4. clearly authorized in writing to undertake these activities on behalf of the unit of government, including submitting the required affidavit.

A form affidavit is reproduced in Appendix 3A.

3.47. Must the building inspector wait for a determination from the licensing board before issuing the building permit?

No. The building inspector is not required to delay issuing the building permit pending the licensing board's review of the local government's affidavit. In fact, if the affidavit appears valid when presented to the building inspector and, based on the information contained in the affidavit along with other information the building inspector might request, the owner appears to be eligible for the exemption, the building inspector does not have a valid legal basis to delay issuing the building permit if all other permit requirements have been met.

3.48. What does the local government do if its building permit is revoked?

If a building permit is revoked, all construction activity must cease, and other permits obtained under state or local laws applicable to the project also may be revoked. The property owner then has three choices: (1) modify its circumstances to become eligible for the exemption, (2) hire a licensed general contractor to superintend the project, or (3) abandon the project altogether. Any resumption of construction activity on the project will require a new building permit (and perhaps other permits applicable to the project).

62. G.S. 153A-362 (for counties) and G.S. 160A-422 (for cities).

3.49. Can the employee or official who executed the affidavit on behalf of the local government delegate the responsibility of supervising the building project to someone else?

No. One of the facts to which the employee or official acting on behalf of the local government must attest in the affidavit is that he or she will personally superintend and manage all aspects of the building construction project and will not delegate this duty to any other person who is not a general contractor licensed in this state. If the individual who executed the affidavit becomes unwilling or unable to personally supervise the project once construction has started, he or she can delegate this responsibility *only* to a general contractor licensed in this state.

3.50. Is an owner-contractor affidavit required for force account work that does not involve a building?

No. The owner-contractor affidavit is only required for construction or repair projects costing $30,000 or more that involve buildings. The affidavit is not required for other types of construction or repair projects undertaken by employees of the local government, such as utility repair work. However, the project must still conform to the dollar limits of the force account statute—the total cost of the labor must be less than $50,000 or the total cost of the project must be less than $125,000 (see section II of Chapter 5 for further discussion of the force account exception).

3.51. Are there any penalties for violating this law?

Yes. If the licensing board determines that the local government was not entitled to claim the owner-contractor exemption, the building inspector must revoke the building permit. If the building construction does not cease or resumes without complying with applicable state laws, G.S. 87-13.1 authorizes the licensing board to apply to superior court for a restraining order and injunction to stop further construction activity, and the court may order the property owner to pay for the board's reasonable costs associated with investigating and prosecuting the violation. Continued construction activity by the property owner also may constitute a violation of the requirements of G.S. 87-1, which is punishable as a Class 2 misdemeanor. In addition, for the employee or official who executes the affidavit on behalf of the local government, swearing falsely on the affidavit (perjury) also is a criminal offense punishable as a Class F felony.

B. Fire Safety Approval for Building Plans

Agencies and persons authorized or directed by law to select plans or erect buildings comprising 20,000 square feet or more for use by counties, cities, and school districts must submit the plans to, and have them approved by, the state commissioner of insurance before they may be received and approved by the governing board or other responsible official on behalf of the local government. The commissioner reviews the plans "as to the safety of the proposed buildings from fire, including the property's occupants or contents."[63] Plans that involve buildings of less than 20,000 square feet, or that do not involve buildings, are not subject to this requirement. Because the statute specifically refers to buildings to be used by counties, cities, and school districts, presumably the requirement does not apply to building construction projects undertaken by other units of local government, such as water and sewer authorities.

C. When Plans Must Be Drawn by an Architect or Engineer; Certificate of Compliance

The plans and specifications for the repair or construction of public buildings must generally be prepared by a registered architect, a registered engineer, or both, if the project exceeds a certain size. The architect or engineer used must be "particularly qualified by training and experience for the type of work involved," and his or her seal, name, and address must be placed on the plans and specifications.[64] In addition, even if state law does not require that the plans and specifications of a particular project be drawn by an architect or engineer, if a design professional does draw the plans, his or her name must be placed on those plans and specifications.[65]

---

63. G.S. 58-31-40(b).
64. G.S. 133-1.1(a).
65. G.S. 133-1.1(e).

3.52. What projects are required to have plans drawn by a licensed architect or engineer?

Under G.S. 133-1.1(a), a licensed architect or engineer is required to draw the plans of the following building construction or repair projects:

1. construction of or additions to a building costing greater than $135,000,
2. repairs that include a major structural change in framing or foundation support systems costing greater than $135,000,
3. repairs that affect "life safety systems" (this term is not defined) costing greater than $100,000,
4. repairs not involving such a major structural change costing more than $300,000.

3.53. Are any projects exempt from the requirement that plans must be drawn by an architect or engineer?

There are five types of projects that, regardless of cost or size, are not required to have plans drawn by a licensed architect or engineer[66] (most of these projects are not likely to be undertaken by a local government). These are

1. dwellings and associated outbuildings (such as barns and private garages),
2. apartment buildings used exclusively as the residence of not more than two families,
3. buildings used for agricultural purposes (other than schools or assembly halls) that are not within the limits of an incorporated municipality,
4. temporary buildings or sheds used exclusively for construction purposes (these buildings cannot be larger than twenty feet in any direction and may not be used for living quarters),
5. pre-engineered garages, sheds, and workshops up to 5,000 square feet used exclusively by city, county, public school, or state employees for purposes related to their employment (these structures must be at least thirty feet from other buildings as well as the property lines of the parcel on which they are built).

3.54. What is a certificate of compliance, and when is it issued?

The architect and/or engineer whose name appears on the plans and specifications must conduct "frequent and regular inspections" or inspections as frequently as required by contract.[67] When satisfied that the contractor has fulfilled the obligations of the plans, specifications, and contract, the architect or engineer is to issue "a signed and sealed certificate of compliance to the awarding authority." The certificate states that (1) the architect's or engineer's inspections have been conducted "with the degree of care and professional skill and judgment ordinarily exercised by a member of that profession" and (2) that in that person's professional opinion and to the best of his or her knowledge, the contractor has fulfilled the obligations of such plans, specifications, and contract. Neither the designer nor the contractor may receive final payment until the local government receives the certificate.[68]

3.55. How does the local government obtain a certificate of compliance if there is no architect or engineer?

If, because of the project's size or a statutory exception, no registered architect or engineer is used, the local government must still obtain a certificate of compliance with the State Building Code. In these instances, the certificate of compliance may be issued by the appropriate city or county inspector(s) or by any licensed architect or engineer.[69] As with projects required to be drawn by an architect or engineer, receipt of a certificate of compliance for these smaller projects is a condition of final payment for the contractor.

The following projects are exempt from the requirement that a certificate of compliance be obtained from the local building inspector or a licensed architect or engineer:

1. the project is exempt from the code;

---

66. G.S. 133-1.1(c).
67. G.S. 133-1.1(b).
68. G.S. 133-1.1(f).
69. G.S. 133-1.1(d).

2. the plans and specifications are approved by the State Construction Office of the North Carolina Department of Administration and the completed project is inspected by the State Construction Office and the state electrical inspector; or
3. the project's total projected cost is less than $100,000 and it does not alter life safety systems.

D. Color Schedules Requirement

G.S. 133-1.1(g) requires that the plans and specifications for building construction and repair projects which must be drawn by a licensed architect or engineer (see section IX.C, above) must include the color schedules for the project if job-installed finishes are part of the project. Projects that are exempt from the requirement that plans and specifications be drawn by a licensed architect or engineer are exempt also from the requirement concerning color schemes.

E. Use of Project Expediters

3.56. What is a project expediter?

G.S. 143-128(e) authorizes local governments, if specified in the bid documents, to assign responsibility for expediting the work on a project to a "single responsible and reliable person, firm, or corporation." This "project expediter" may be either one of the prime contractors or someone else. The designation of a project expediter is optional; the local government may choose to designate one if it wishes regardless of the size or estimated cost of the project. A project expediter is most commonly used when a project is contracted under the separate-prime method since there are multiple prime contractors involved in the project. However, the use of a project expediter is not limited to separate-prime projects.

3.57. What are the responsibilities of a project expediter?

The project expediter's function is to expedite the work on a project—in other words, to keep the project on schedule. He or she may be given responsibility for preparing the project schedule, and if so, the statute requires that he or she allow all contractors and subcontractors performing any of the four branches of work for which separate specifications must be drawn on building construction projects costing over $300,000—HVAC, electrical, plumbing, and general—to have "equal input" in preparing the initial schedule. In carrying out his or her responsibilities, the project expediter may recommend to the local government whether payment to a particular contractor should be approved.

Appendix 3A Owner Exemption Affidavit

STATE OF NORTH CAROLINA

COUNTY OF _______________

OWNER EXEMPTION AFFIDAVIT
PURSUANT TO G.S. 87-14(a)(1)

_____________________ Inspections Department

Address and Parcel Identification of Real Property Where Building is to be Constructed or Altered:

____.

I, ____,
(Print Full Name)

hereby claim an exemption from licensure under G.S. 87-1(b)(2) by initialing the relevant provision in paragraph 1 and initialing paragraphs 2-4 below and attesting to the following:

1. ______ I certify that I am the owner of the property set forth above on which this building is to be constructed or altered;

   OR

   _____ I am legally authorized to act on behalf of the firm or corporation which is constructing or altering this building on the property owned by the firm or corporation as set forth above (name of firm or corporation:____);

2. ________ I will personally superintend and manage all aspects of the construction or alternation of the building and that duty will not be delegated to any person not duly licensed under the terms of Article 1 of Chapter 87 of the General Statutes of North Carolina;

3. ________ I will be personally present for all inspections required by the North Carolina State Building Code, unless the plans for the construction or alteration of the building were drawn and sealed by an architect licensed pursuant to Chapter 83A of the General Statutes of North Carolina;

4. ________ I understand that a copy of this AFFIDAVIT will be transmitted to the North Carolina Licensing Board for General Contractors for verification that I am validly entitled to claim an exemption under G.S. 87-1(b)(2) for the building construction or alteration specified herein. I further understand that, if the North Carolina Licensing Board for General Contractors determines that I was not entitled to claim this exemption, the building permit issued for the building construction or alteration specified herein shall be revoked pursuant to G.S. 153A-362 or G.S. 160A-422.

____ ________________
(Signature of Affiant) Date

Sworn to (or affirmed) and Subscribed before me
this the ___ day of ____________________, 20__

____
Signature of Notary Public

____
Printed Name of Notary Public

My Commission Expires:________________ (Notary Stamp or Seal)

(NOTE: It is a Class F felony to willfully commit perjury in any affidavit taken pursuant to law—G.S. 14-209)

Chapter 4

Historically Underutilized Business (HUB) Participation Requirements

Chapter 4

Historically Underutilized Business (HUB) Participation Requirements

I. Introduction

Since 1989, state law has required units of local government to employ measures designed to promote the participation of minority businesses (eventually referred to as historically underutilized businesses, or "HUB") in certain public building construction projects.[1]

It is important to note that North Carolina law has *never established or mandated specific quotas or set-asides* for HUB participation; rather, it has established procedures designed to *promote and facilitate* HUB participation. In fact, state law specifically requires that public building contracts, including those subject to informal and formal competitive bidding requirements and those awarded under the construction management at-risk building method, shall be awarded "without regard to race, religion, color, creed, national origin, sex, age, or handicapping condition."[2] In addition, state law also specifies that contracting authorities (including contractors and subcontractors) are not required to enter into contracts with HUBs that are not the lowest responsive, responsible bidders, the standard of award for contracts in the informal and formal bidding ranges.[3] In short, HUB participation requirements do not override the competitive bidding standard of award. And, while intended to rectify past discrimination, HUB participation requirements are not to be construed to now mandate discrimination (or, rather, reverse discrimination) in public contracting.

II. Definition of HUB

North Carolina law defines a "historically underutilized business," or "HUB," as a business that is at least 51 percent owned (or, in the case of a corporation, at least 51 percent of the stock is owned) and day-to-day management and daily business operations are controlled by one or more citizens or lawful permanent residents who are members of a minority or socially and economically disadvantaged group. A "minority person" is a member of one or more of the following demographic groups:

1. *Black*—a person having origins in any of the black racial groups of Africa;

---

1. Minority participation goals for certain building construction contracts were enacted by the N.C. General Assembly in June 1989 (S.L. 1989-490), presumably in response to the U.S. Supreme Court's landmark decision in *Croson* decided in January of that year. City of Richmond v. J.A. Croson Co., 109 S. Ct. 706 (1989).

2. Section 143-128.2(h) of the North Carolina General Statutes (hereinafter G.S.).

3. *Id.*

2. *Hispanic*—a person of Spanish or Portuguese culture having origins in Mexico, South or Central America, or the Caribbean islands, regardless of race;
3. *Asian American*—a person having origins in any of the original peoples of the Far East, Southeast Asia, Asia, Indian continent, or Pacific islands;
4. *American Indian*—a person having origins in any of the original Indian peoples of North America;
5. *Female*;
6. *Disabled*—a person with a disability as defined in Sections 168-1 or 168A-3 of the North Carolina General Statutes (hereinafter G.S.).[4]

A "socially and economically disadvantaged person" is someone who qualifies as such under federal law.[5]

While the terms *minority-owned business* or *M/WBE* (minority- and women-owned business enterprise) are commonly used, North Carolina law generally defines all these businesses, especially minority-owned businesses, as "historically underutilized businesses."[6] To be consistent with North Carolina law, this book uses the term *historically underutilized business*, or *HUB*, when referring to North Carolina statutory requirements.

III. General Requirements

A. Categories of HUB Requirements

HUB participation requirements fall into three general categories, as follows:

1. *setting goals* for HUB participation in building construction and repair contracting,
2. *engaging in good faith efforts* to solicit HUB participation in the bidding process for building construction and repair projects, and
3. *reporting* HUB participation activities and efforts.

These requirements vary depending on the cost and funding source of the building construction project. Smaller cost projects are subject to some requirements for the unit of local government; larger cost projects are subject to greater requirements for both local governments as well as bidders.

B. Projects to which HUB Requirements Apply

Under state law, HUB requirements apply to construction and repair projects involving *buildings* in the formal and informal competitive bidding ranges (see section II of Chapter 3 for further discussion of the definition of a building). Informal HUB requirements apply to building construction projects costing $30,000 up to $300,000. Formal HUB requirements apply to projects costing $300,000 or more.

It is important to note an inconsistent overlap in the statutory requirements for HUB participation in building construction projects costing between $300,000 and $500,000. While one statute (G.S. 143-131) imposes informal HUB requirements on construction projects in the informal bidding range—which extends to projects costing up to $500,000—another statute (G.S. 143-128.2) imposes *formal* HUB requirements on building projects costing *$300,000* or more. For projects costing between $300,000 and $500,000, the safest course of action is to follow the more stringent requirements of G.S. 143-128.2 even though these projects are subject to only informal competitive bidding requirements. It is for this reason that many local governments apply formal bidding requirements to building construction projects in this range.

Because state law limits HUB participation efforts to building construction or repair projects subject to competitive bidding requirements, HUB requirements do not apply to building construction or repair projects costing

4. G.S. 143-128.4(a) & (b). *See also* N.C. Office for Historically Underutilized Businesses FAQs, www.doa.state.nc.us/hub/faq.aspx.

5. G.S. 143-128.4(b)(7); 15 U.S.C. § 637(a)(5).

6. G.S. 143-128.4(a1).

Table 4.1 Basic HUB Requirements under North Carolina Law

Estimated Total Project Cost	Competitive Bidding Requirements	HUB Requirements
Below $30,000	None	None
$30,000 to $300,000	Informal bidding (G.S. 143-131)	Informal HUB (G.S. 143-131)[a]
$300,000 or more	Informal bidding (G.S. 143-131)	Formal HUB (G.S. 143-128.2)
$500,000 or more	Formal bidding (G.S. 143-129)	Formal HUB (G.S. 143-128.2)

Note: See Appendix 4A for a checklist of specific informal and formal requirements for HUB participation.

a. For projects costing $100,000 or more and funded wholly or in part with state funds, state law requires the local government to use a 10 percent goal, unless the local government has previously established and maintained another verifiable goal.

less than $30,000 or to any construction or repair projects not involving public buildings regardless of cost, unless required under the terms of state or federal grant funding. In addition, HUB requirements do not apply to any other type of local government contract, including purchase and service contracts (again, unless required under the terms of state or federal grant funding).

Sometimes federal and state grant requirements apply minority participation requirements to construction projects that do not involve buildings. In these instances, minority participation requirements must be complied with regardless of the nature of the construction project (see section IX of this chapter for further discussion of federally funded projects).[7] The basic HUB requirements under North Carolina law are presented in Table 4.1.

IV. HUB Participation Goals

As stated above, North Carolina's HUB program is aspirational, not a quota or set-aside system. As such, local governments are required to establish percentage goals for participation by historically underutilized businesses in public building construction projects (meaning the percent of work to be performed by HUBs). What percentage goals apply to which types of building construction projects depends on the cost of the project and the source of funding.

A. State-Funded Projects

For state-funded projects costing $100,000 or more, the state has a verifiable HUB participation goal of 10 percent of the total project value for each *state* building project, including building projects done by a private entity on a facility to be leased or purchased by the state. If an entity, whether public or private (including local governments), receives appropriations or grant funds from the state for a construction project with a cost of $100,000 or more, the entity must have a verifiable 10 percent HUB participation goal in the total value of the work on that project. If the local government adopted a different verifiable goal prior to December 1, 2001, the local government unit may apply its local goal to the project if it had and continues to have a sufficiently strong basis in evidence to justify the use of that goal.[8]

The 10 percent state goal requirement applies to the "total value of work" of a specific building construction project costing $100,000 or more. This does not mean that the amount of state funds contributed to the project must equal or exceed $100,000; rather, it is the total cost of the project that triggers the requirement. Presumably, this means that a contribution of *any* amount of state funds to the project will trigger the requirement if the total

7. *See* Opinion of the Attorney General to Mr. John T. Carter Jr., Jacksonville city attorney (July 18, 2002), www.ncdoj.gov/About-DOJ/Legal-Services/Legal-Opinions/Opinions/City-of-Jacksonville-Wastewater-Collection-Facilit.aspx.

8. G.S. 143-128.2(a).

project cost is $100,000 or more. For example, a project costing $500,000 that is funded in part with a $50,000 grant from the state must comply with the state HUB participation goal requirement of 10 percent.

It is important to note that the requirement is based on the *total project cost*, not the cost of *individual contracts* that constitute the total project. For example, if a building renovation project consists of three individual contracts (such as plumbing, HVAC, and general) each costing $75,000, the requirement would still apply because the total project cost is $225,000. Even though the individual contracts are all less than $100,000, the total cost of the project exceeds the $100,000 threshold, thus triggering the requirement.

B. Locally Funded Projects

For locally funded projects costing $300,000 or more, local governments must adopt an "appropriate verifiable percentage goal" for HUB participation in the "total value of work" for all building construction projects costing $300,000 or more if the project is funded entirely with nonstate funds.[9] As with the 10 percent state goal requirement, the local goal requirement is based on the cost of the "total value of work," not the cost of individual contracts.

C. Building Projects to Which Goals Do Not Apply

For all building construction projects, if the project is funded in whole or in part with state funds and costs less than $100,000, or if the project is funded entirely with non-state funds and costs less than $300,000, state law does not require HUB participation goals. In addition, HUB participation goals are not required for the purchase and erection of prefabricated buildings (though HUB participation requirements would apply to on-site construction work, such as constructing foundations).[10]

D. Establishing HUB Goals

HUB participation requirements are based on "appropriate, verifiable goals" adopted by the local government. The HUB statutes do not define what constitutes an "appropriate, verifiable goal"; they merely provide minimal procedural requirements for adopting the goals (namely, that the local government must adopt its goals after notice and public hearing).[11] However, a number of federal court decisions have articulated a set of legal requirements for constitutionally valid HUB goals.[12]

When the government uses a racial classification, that classification is subject to the strict scrutiny standard of judicial review regardless of whether the program seeks to benefit minority groups.[13] Strict scrutiny is applied even if the race-based program merely establishes aspirational goals as opposed to quotas or set-asides; that race is the basis for the classification is sufficient to trigger the highest level of judicial scrutiny.[14] In order to satisfy strict scrutiny and enable the court to uphold its minority business participation program, the local government must demonstrate (1) a "compelling interest 'in remedying the effects of past or present racial discrimination'"[15] and (2) that the program is narrowly tailored to serve the government's compelling interest.[16] While some have argued that the "good faith efforts" requirements under the statute do not create a preference and are thus race neutral, a

---

9. *Id.*

10. G.S. 143-128.2(j).

11. G.S. 143-128.2(a).

12. For more information on the constitutional requirements and limitations on HUB programs see Norma R. Houston and Jessica Jansepar Ross, HUB Participation in Building Construction Contracting by N.C. Local Governments: Statutory Requirements and Constitutional Limitations, Local Gov't L. Bull. No. 131 (Feb. 2013).

13. Richmond v. J.A. Croson Co., 488 U.S. 469, 493–94 (1989) (plurality opinion); Adarand Constructors, Inc. v. Pena (*Adarand* III), 515 U.S. 200 (1995) (applying strict scrutiny to review of federal programs with racial classifications).

14. DynaLantic Corp. v. U.S. Dep't of Def., 885 F. Supp. 2d 237, 281 (2012) (quoting *Adarand* III, 515 U.S. at 205, 223–27) ("Defendants fail to recognize, however, that the Supreme Court explicitly adopted the *Croson* standards in *Adarand* III, a case involving race-based 'goals' as opposed to 'quotas.'").

15. *Id.* at 241 (quoting Shaw v. Hunt, 517 U.S. 899, 909 (1996)).

16. *Id.* at 242 (citing Alexander v. Estepp, 95 F.3d 312, 315 (4th Cir. 1996)).

review of cases decided around the country suggests that if challenged, a decision to reject a bid for failure to meet the good faith efforts requirement would probably be subject to strict scrutiny.

To meet these constitutional requirements, many jurisdictions, including several North Carolina local governments and the State of North Carolina, have conducted disparity studies to document the history of discrimination in the construction industry as well as the underutilization of minority businesses by the public agencies themselves. Local governments are not required to have disparity studies, but such studies may support the constitutionality of a local government's HUB goals and program.

Greatly simplified, a disparity study evaluates the past contracting practices of a local government that proposes to establish HUB goals and participation efforts, the market area from which the contractors doing business with the unit are drawn, and the availability of qualified HUB contractors within that market area in the trades used by the local government. The study then analyzes whether there is a statistically significant disparity between the firms available to and those used by the local government, attempting to control for race-neutral factors such as firm size and experience. A disparity study also evaluates anecdotal evidence and statistical evidence, where available, of discrimination in the local marketplace to determine if the governmental unit has been a passive participant in industry-wide discrimination. Evidence may be drawn from census data, the records of the unit being studied, federal studies, public hearings, surveys, and interviews. A number of private consulting firms have developed expertise in conducting disparity studies. The studies can be costly (ranging from $50,000 to hundreds of thousands of dollars, depending on the size of the unit), time consuming, and demanding for local government staff.

Local government officials are advised to develop or obtain information about the availability and local utilization of minority contractors in their particular areas in order to establish supportable goals. Public agencies should consider developing separate goals for the different categories of HUB firms, as defined under the statute, and for different types of work, since the availability of HUB firms varies according to the type of contract involved. Information from statewide or other local government disparity studies may help support a particular jurisdiction's goal.

V. Good Faith Efforts

In addition to adopting HUB participation goals, local governments and, in some instances bidders, must engage in efforts to recruit HUB participation in certain building construction projects. As with participation goals, these participation efforts vary depending on the cost and funding source of the project.

A. Informal HUB Good Faith Efforts

For building construction and repair projects in the informal bidding range costing between $30,000 and $300,000, local governments must

1. solicit HUB participation in contracts,
2. document efforts to recruit HUB participation,
3. maintain a record of HUB contractors solicited, and
4. report all data on HUB participation efforts to the N.C. Office for Historically Underutilized Businesses.[17]

No statutory requirements are imposed on bidders and contractors involved in informal bidding projects. Only the local government is required to comply with these informal HUB requirements.

The statute does not define what types of informal solicitation efforts local governments must utilize; most local governments use their HUB outreach plan (adopted for formal HUB requirements) to satisfy the need to solicit HUB participation on building construction projects costing between $30,000 and $300,000.

17. G.S. 143-131(b).

B. Formal HUB Good Faith Efforts—Local Government

For building construction and repair projects costing $300,000 and more, good faith efforts to encourage minority business participation apply to both local governments and bidders.

The local government must establish its good faith efforts prior to bid solicitation. Its good faith efforts must include the following steps:

1. develop a HUB outreach plan to identify businesses that engage in public building projects and implement outreach efforts to encourage participation in these projects (efforts can include such activities as education, recruitment, and interaction between minority and nonminority businesses);
2. attend scheduled pre-bid conferences and explain minority goals;
3. notify interested HUBs of the opportunity to bid on a project at least ten days prior to bid opening (even though the required advertising period for formal construction projects is only seven days and no formal advertising is required for projects in the informal bidding range); the advertisement must include a description of the work as well as state the date, time, and location where bids are to be submitted, the public entity's contact person for the project, where bid documents can be reviewed, and any special requirements for the project;
4. advertise the project through media outlets likely to inform HUBs of the opportunity to bid;
5. maintain documentation of any contacts, correspondence, or conversation with minority firms in an attempt to meet goals;
6. review HUB participation requirements with the project designer prior to recommendation of the contract award;
7. evaluate bidder's documentation to determine that good faith efforts required of the bidder have been satisfied;
8. provide relevant documentation to the State Construction Office and the N.C. Office for Historically Underutilized Businesses upon request and satisfy all HUB Office reporting requirements.[18]

It is important to note that the local government's good faith requirements are *in addition* to other competitive bidding and public contracting requirements mandated under state law and established by local policy.

C. Formal HUB Good Faith Efforts—Bidders

The local government must also require bidders to make good faith efforts to encourage HUB participation in their bids, including the ten specific actions listed in the statute.[19] Under G.S. 143-128.2(f), the good faith efforts for contractors include

1. contacting minority businesses to submit a quote at least 10 days before the bid deadline;
2. making specifications and plans available for review by prospective minority businesses;
3. breaking down or combining elements of work into economically feasible units to facilitate minority participation;
4. working with minority trade, community, or contractor organizations identified by the Office of Historically Underutilized Businesses;
5. attending any prebid meetings scheduled by the local government;
6. providing assistance in getting required bonding or insurance or providing alternatives to bonding or insurance for subcontractors;
7. negotiating in good faith with interested minority businesses;

---

18. G.S. 143-128.2(e); N.C. Admin. Code (hereinafter N.C.A.C.) tit. 1, ch. 301, § .0306(a).
19. G.S. 143-128.2(f).

8. providing assistance to an otherwise qualified minority business in need of equipment, loan capital, lines of credit, or joint pay agreements to secure loans, supplies, or letters of credit, including waiving credit that is ordinarily required;
9. negotiating joint venture and partnership arrangements with minority businesses in order to increase opportunities for their participation; and
10. providing quick pay agreements and policies to enable minority contractors and suppliers to meet cash-flow demands.

The N.C. Office for Historically Underutilized Businesses assigns points to be awarded for compliance with this statutory list.[20] Each action can be assigned up to ten points, and no contractor can be required to earn more than fifty points. While bidders must make good faith efforts to solicit HUB participation, the level of minority participation in bidders' bids does *not* affect the contract award decision. The lowest responsive, responsible bidder standard of award still applies regardless of the level of minority participation. However, failure to submit required documents of good faith efforts or to make sufficient good faith efforts renders the bid nonresponsive.

Some documentation requirements apply to all bidders while additional requirements are imposed on the apparent low bidder. When submitting a bid, all contractors must identify *on their bid* the HUB businesses to be used on the project and include an affidavit listing the bidder's good faith efforts to solicit HUB participation and the total dollar value of work to be performed by HUBs.[21] This requirement applies even if the prime contractor is itself a HUB. Failure to satisfy these documentation requirements renders the bid nonresponsive, and the unit of government must reject it. Once the apparent low bidder is selected and prior to the awarding of the contract, the contractor must submit either an affidavit describing the percentage of HUB work to be performed which is equal to or greater than the local government's minority participation goal or documentation of the bidder's good faith efforts to meet the local government's HUB participation goal.[22] Within thirty days after contract award, the winning bidder must submit a list of all subcontractors to be used on the project.[23]

D. When Bids May or May Not Be Rejected Due to Good Faith Efforts

While failure to submit statutorily required information and documentation renders a bid nonresponsive, a bidder's failure to actually hire HUB firms is not. A bidder who has complied with all good faith efforts requirements and submitted an affidavit to this effect, but indicates on his bid that he has no HUB subcontractors, has still submitted a responsive bid. Similarly, a bidder whose percentage of HUB participation on his bid is less than the percentage goals set by the local government has still submitted a responsive bid. Neither of these scenarios provides a legal justification for rejecting the bid or failing to award the contract if the bidder is otherwise the lowest responsive, responsible bidder.

G.S. 143-128.2 makes clear that contract awards are to be made "without regard to race, religion, color, creed, national origin, sex, age, or handicapping condition," and that nothing in that statute is to be "construed to require contractors or awarding authorities to award contracts or subcontracts to or to make purchases of materials or equipment from minority-business contractors or minority-business subcontractors who do not submit the lowest responsible, responsive bid or bids."[24] This language makes clear that local governments and contractors are *not* required to make awards to or purchases from any bidder other than the lowest responsible, responsive bidder or bidders in order to meet minority participation goals. Indeed, local governments are *prohibited* from making contract awards on any basis other than to the lowest responsible, responsive bidder. Nor can local governments require a bidder to modify or increase that bidder's level of HUB participation.

---

20. 1 N.C.A.C. 301 .0102.

21. G.S. 143-128.2(c). If a bidder proposes to perform *all* of the work with its own forces (employees) in lieu of hiring subcontractors, it can submit an affidavit to this effect in lieu of the HUB participation affidavit.

22. G.S. 143-128.2(c)(1).

23. Sample HUB participation affidavits are available on the N.C. State Construction Office website; click link to Minority Business Participation Form, www.nc-sco.com/docBidding.aspx.

24. G.S. 143-128.2(h).

VI. Reporting HUB Participation Efforts

The third HUB participation requirement to which local governments must adhere is reporting their HUB participation efforts. For building construction and repair projects subject to HUB participation requirements, local governments must report certain information related to these projects to the N.C. Office for Historically Underutilized Businesses. As with participation goals and good faith efforts, reporting requirements vary depending on the cost of the project. These reports must be submitted in the format and contain the data prescribed by the secretary of administration.[25] Personnel in the N.C. Office for Historically Underutilized Businesses provide training and are available to assist local governments in learning how to use the HUBSCO reporting system.

A. Informal HUB Projects

For building construction or repair contracts costing between $30,000 and $300,000, local governments must report the following information on each project upon completion of that project using the HUBSCO Informal Project Report Form:

1. type of project,
2. total dollar value of the project,
3. dollar value of minority business participation in each project, and
4. documentation of efforts to recruit minority participation.[26]

B. Formal HUB Projects

For building construction or repair projects costing $300,000 or more, local governments must report semiannually the following information on each project using the HUBSCO Formal Project Report Form:

1. the verifiable percentage goal for the project;
2. the type and total dollar value of the project;
3. HUB utilization by
    a. minority business category,
    b. trade,
    c. total dollar value of contracts awarded to each minority group for each project,
    d. applicable good faith effort guidelines or rules used to recruit minority business participation, and
    e. good faith documentation accepted by the public entity from the successful bidder;
4. utilization, as both prime contractors and subcontractors, of minority businesses under the various construction methods listed under G.S. 143-128(a1), which are single-prime, separate-prime (also referred to as multi-prime), dual-bidding, construction management at-risk, and any alternative contracting methods approved by the state building commission or authorized by the General Assembly in a local act.[27]

The HUB requirements under North Carolina law discussed in the preceding sections are summarized in Table 4.2.

VII. Becoming HUB Certified

All businesses that seek to qualify as a HUB must be certified through the Statewide Uniform Certification Program administered by the N.C. Office for Historically Underutilized Businesses. A business wishing to become HUB Certified may apply free of charge to the N.C. Office for Historically Underutilized Businesses, and personnel

---

25. G.S. 143-128.3(a).

26. G.S. 143-131(b). The HUBSCO Informal Project Report Form is available on the N.C. Office for Historically Underutilized Businesses website under "Certification Forms and Documents," www.doa.state.nc.us/hub/forms.aspx.

27. *Id.* The HUBSCO Formal Project Report Form is available on the N.C. Office for Historically Underutilized Businesses website under "Certification Forms and Documents," www.doa.state.nc.us/hub/forms.aspx.

Table 4.2 Summary of HUB Requirements under North Carolina Law

Project Cost	Goals	Good Faith Efforts	Reporting
Below $30,000	Not required	Not required	Not required
$30,000 to $300,000	Not required (unless $100,000 or more and funded with state funds[a])	*Local Government:* Informal solicitation *Bidders:* No requirements	*Local Government:* Informal reporting to HUB Office
$300,000 and above	Required	*Local Government:* Formal outreach and good faith efforts *Bidders:* Formal good faith efforts	*Local Government:* Formal reporting to HUB Office

a. For projects costing $100,000 or more and funded wholly or in part with state funds, state law requires the local government to use a 10 percent goal, unless the local government has previously established and maintained another verifiable goal.

in that office are available to assist businesses with the certification process. When applying for certification, the business must provide documentation that demonstrates ownership, management, and control of the company by a minority, a woman, a disabled or a socially and economically disadvantaged individual or group of individuals as required by state law. Once awarded, certification remains effective for four years provided the business remains eligible for HUB designation.

Only businesses certified through this program count toward a local government's HUB participation percentage goal.[28] However, lack of HUB certification does not preclude a business or firm from submitting a bid to a state or local government entity, nor can lack of HUB certification be considered by the local government in making a contract award decision.

VIII. Sanctions

A public entity may be subject to penalties for failing to comply with statutory requirements for minority business participation programs[29] as well as face significant costs if the constitutionality of its goals program is challenged in court.[30]

A. Statutory Penalties

Failure to meet the statutory requirements for goal setting and good faith efforts under G.S. 143-128.2 can result in a loss of time, money, and even the ability to bid contracts without Department of Administration (DOA) and attorney general pre-approval.[31] If a public entity has failed to meet the requirements established in G.S. 143-128.2 for any of its projects, the secretary of the DOA can require the entity to implement a corrective plan to address whatever deficiencies the secretary has identified.[32] The corrective plan should apply to the current project to the extent feasible but also may apply to future building construction projects.[33]

28. G.S. 143-128.4(e). More information on this program is available at the website for the N.C. Office for Historically Underutilized Businesses, www.doa.state.nc.us/hub.

29. G.S. 143-128.3(b); *see generally* G.S. 143-128.2 (detailing statutory requirements for HUB participation goals).

30. *See* H.B. Rowe. Co., Inc. v. Conti, No. 5:03-cv-00278-BO, ¶ 8 (E.D.N.C. 2011) (amended judgment awarding attorneys' fees to plaintiff).

31. *See* G.S. 143-128.3(b)(1)–(2).

32. G.S. 143-128.3(b).

33. *Id.*

If the public entity does not file a corrective plan after being notified by the secretary, or submits a plan that is not in accordance with the secretary's terms, the secretary can

1. require the entity to consult with the DOA HUB Office to create a new corrective plan subject to approval by the secretary and the attorney general[34] and/or
2. restrict for up to a year the public entity's ability to bid contracts under G.S. 143-128 without the secretary's and the attorney general's pre-approval of the entity's good faith compliance plan for each project.[35]

B. Litigation Costs and Penalties

Litigating a constitutional challenge to a minority business participation program is often costly and time consuming. Generally, these challenges are brought by contractors (or their respective associations) who lost a bid on a building contract for not meeting either minority participation or good faith effort goals and who believe that the entity's policy violates the Equal Protection Clause of the Fourteenth Amendment to the U.S. Constitution.[36] Not everyone who disagrees with the policy can challenge it; the plaintiff must have been injured by the policy.[37] While it is difficult to predict with certainty what remedies a judge will require, recent case law gives some indication of possible costs. In *H.B. Rowe, Co., Inc. v. Tippett,* the Fourth Circuit Court of Appeals upheld the Department of Transportation's (DOT) minority business participation program as it applied to African Americans and Native Americans[38] but determined it was unconstitutional as applied to other minorities because there was not enough statistical evidence of discrimination.[39] Because part of the program was found to be unconstitutional, DOT was required to pay the plaintiff's reasonable attorneys' fees, in addition to its own litigation costs.[40]

IX. Federal Minority-Business Enterprise Participation Requirements

Cities and counties (but not other local governmental units) are authorized by G.S. 160A-17.1(3a) to "[a]gree to and comply with minimum minority business enterprise participation requirements established by the federal government and its agencies in projects financed by federal grants-in-aid or loans." Such requirements may be included in project specifications, and contracts may be awarded under the applicable formal or informal bidding procedure "to the lowest responsible bidder or bidders meeting these and any other specifications." This provision is part of a broad authorization to make contracts and accept grants-in-aid and loans from the federal and state governments and their agencies for constructing, expanding, maintaining, and operating any project or facility or performing any function that the city or county is legally authorized to provide or perform.

---

34. G.S. 143-128.3(b)(1).

35. G.S. 143-128.3(b)(2).

36. *See generally* Richmond v. J.A. Croson Co., 488 U.S. 469, 483 (1989); H.B. Rowe Co., Inc. v. Tippett, 615 F.3d 233, 238 (4th Cir. 2010).

37. *See* Md. Hwy. Contractors Ass'n, Inc. v. Maryland, 933 F.2d 1246, 1250–52 (contractors' association could not bring challenge to minority business enterprise statute where neither the association, nor any of its members, had been injured by the statute). In order to bring a claim, a party "must be able to demonstrate a 'distinct and palpable injury' that is likely to be redressed if the requested relief is granted." *Id.* at 1250 (quoting Valley Forge Coll. v. Ams. United, 454 U.S. 464, 488 (1982)).

38. *Rowe*, 615 F.3d at 257.

39. *See id.* at 251 n.8.

40. *See supra* note 30.

Appendix 4A HUB Participation Program Checklist

I. HUB Participation Goals

A. Covered Projects

- ❏ building construction or repair
- ❏ $100,000 or more and funded in part or whole with state funds (10% goal or local goal established prior to 12/1/2001)
- ❏ $300,000 or more and funded with local funds (goal established by local government)

B. Statutory Requirements

- ❏ verifiable goal
- ❏ adopted after public hearing
- ❏ governing board approval

C. Constitutional Requirements

- ❏ Compelling governmental interest in remedying past and current discrimination proven by
  - ❏ significant statistical disparity
  - ❏ between availability of qualified, willing, and able minority contractors
  - ❏ and utilization of these firms in the public and private sector
  - ❏ in the unit of government's market area
  - ❏ that has been validated as resulting from discrimination
  - ❏ and is corroborated by anecdotal evidence.
- ❏ Program is narrowly tailored to achieve compelling governmental interest by
  - ❏ considering workable, race-neutral alternatives,
  - ❏ evaluating continuing need and duration of policy,
  - ❏ ensuring goals are related to percentage of minority-owned firms in relevant market area,
  - ❏ providing for flexibility in the policy,
  - ❏ limiting the burden on third parties,
  - ❏ Avoiding over-inclusiveness.

II. Good Faith Efforts

A. Informal Requirements (projects costing between $30,000–$300,000)

Local government must

- ❏ solicit HUB participation in contracts,
- ❏ document efforts to recruit HUB participation,
- ❏ maintain a record of HUB contractors solicited, and
- ❏ report all data on HUB participation efforts to the N.C. Office for Historically Underutilized Businesses.

B. Formal Requirements (projects costing $300,000 or more)

Local government must

- ❏ develop HUB outreach plan,
- ❏ attend scheduled pre-bid meetings,
- ❏ notify interested HUBs of bidding opportunity at least ten days prior to bid opening,
- ❏ advertise projects through media outlets likely to inform HUBs of bidding opportunity,
- ❏ maintain documentation of contacts with HUBs in attempt to meet goals,
- ❏ review HUB participation requirements with project designer prior to contract award recommendation,
- ❏ evaluate bidder's documents to determine bidder good faith efforts requirements are satisfied,
- ❏ satisfy HUB reporting requirements.

All bidders must

- ❏ identify on their bids the HUB businesses used on the project,
- ❏ submit with bids an affidavit listing good faith efforts to solicit HUB participation and total dollar value of work by HUBs; local governments may not require bidders to earn more than fifty points in good faith efforts.

Apparent low bidder must

- ❏ submit affidavit describing percentage of HUB work compared to unit's HUB goals or
- ❏ document good faith efforts to meet local goals;
- ❏ list all subcontractors on the project.

III. Reporting Requirements

A. Informal Requirements (projects costing between $30,000–$300,000)

Report to the NC HUB Office upon completion of each project

- ❏ type of project
- ❏ total dollar value of project
- ❏ dollar value of minority business participation on each project
- ❏ documentation of efforts to recruit minority participation

B. Formal Requirements (projects costing $300,000 or more)

Report to the N.C. HUB office semi-annually

- ❏ the verifiable percentage goal for the project
- ❏ the type and total dollar value of the project
- ❏ minority business (HUB) utilization by
  - ❏ minority business category,
  - ❏ trade,
  - ❏ total dollar value of contracts awarded to each minority group for each project,
  - ❏ applicable good faith effort guidelines or rules used to recruit minority business participation, and
  - ❏ good faith documentation accepted by the public entity from the successful bidder.
- ❏ Utilization of minority businesses under the various construction methods authorized under state law

Chapter 5

Exceptions to Competitive Bidding Requirements

Chapter 5

Exceptions to Competitive Bidding Requirements

This chapter outlines the exceptions to competitive bidding requirements for construction and repair contracts entered into by North Carolina local governments. Omitted are those exceptions to the competitive bidding rules that relate only to the purchase of apparatus, supplies, materials, or equipment (purchase contracts). If a contract entered into under an exception to competitive bidding requirements is challenged, the local government entering into such a contract has the burden of showing that the exception applies.[1]

It is important to note that, where an exception to competitive bidding requirements applies, the local government is not *required* to use it. Local governments may always choose to follow competitive bidding procedures even if an exception is available. If a local government is uncertain as to whether a particular situation falls squarely within the legal requirements of a particular exception, the better course of action is to follow the applicable competitive bidding procedures.

I. Change Orders

The construction process is dynamic. Changes in plans in response to unanticipated difficulties or opportunities are not uncommon during a construction project. Most construction contracts provide, through the use of change orders or other mechanisms, for incorporating into the contract any additional or different work that may be required during construction.

A local government may make changes in or additions to a construction or repair project during the course of work without having to bid the changes or additions as long as the original contract was entered into in compliance with competitive bidding requirements.[2] This exception, involving what are commonly called "change orders," applies to projects in both the formal and informal bidding ranges.

5.1. Must the governing board approve change orders?

Change orders or other contractual modifications describing additional or altered work must be approved by the local government, though approval by the governing board itself is not required regardless of the cost of the original contract or the cost of the change order. Because a change order is considered an exception to competitive

1. *See* Raynor v. Comm'rs for the Town of Louisburg, 220 N.C. 348 (1941).
2. Section 143-129(3)(4) of the North Carolina General Statutes (hereinafter G.S.).

bidding requirements, the formalities required for the original contract are not required for a change order under that contract so long as the original contract was properly bid. However, the change order must be approved by an employee or agent of the local government who is authorized to do so, and this individual should be named in the original contract. Typically, the terms and conditions of the contract will require approval by both the project architect or engineer and a local government official, such as the construction manager or the finance officer.

It is important to keep in mind that the local government's appropriation for the construction project must include a sufficient sum for contingencies to cover any increased costs resulting from the proposed change. If a change order results in the need to increase the total appropriation for the project the governing board must approve the budget amendment, and preaudit requirements will apply (see section II of Chapter 1 for further discussion of preaudit requirements).

5.2. Must all change orders be in writing?

Although the change order exception itself does not require change orders to be in writing, the terms and conditions of the construction contract may do so, and in this instance, oral change orders are not legally valid or enforceable.[3] Even absent a term or condition in the contract requiring change orders to be in writing, a change order, as a modification of the contract, is, in essence, a new contract, thus necessitating that the change order be put in writing. In addition, if the change in scope of work results in an increase in the total cost of the contract, the change order is subject to the preaudit requirements of Section 159-28 of the North Carolina General Statutes (hereinafter G.S.), including that a preaudit certificate be affixed to the written document incurring the fiscal obligation on the local government, thus necessitating a written change order (see section II of Chapter 1 for further discussion of the preaudit requirement).

5.3. Under what circumstances is a change order legally valid?

It is important that change orders be reserved for changes in circumstances that arise *after* the work is under way and that were *not* anticipated when the project was originally bid. If a local government knows before it enters into the contract that the specifications are inaccurate or that changes will be needed, the specifications should be revised and the project rebid. Under no circumstances should a change order be used to allow the contractor to correct an error or omission in the original bid. The local government should deny approval of a change order that it believes is not legally valid.

Sometimes the determination as to whether a change order is valid will depend on the terms and conditions of the contract and the bid specifications. For example, a change order requesting permission to remove borrow soil without seeding and landscaping the borrow area was properly denied when the contract specifically required seeding and landscaping of borrow areas.[4] Similarly, a change order requesting payment for additional excavation beyond that stated in the specifications was properly denied,[5] as was a change order requesting compensation for work that was contemplated within the original lump sum contract.[6] On the other hand, a change order requesting additional compensation resulting from delays in the project due to no fault of the contractor was held valid,[7] as was a change order requesting compensation for additional time required to excavate rock due to a mutual mistake by both parties in estimating the amount of rock to be excavated.[8]

---

3. Brokers, Inc. v. High Point City Bd. of Ed., 33 N.C. App. 24, 29 (1977). However, if both parties, by their conduct, waive the requirements of a contract, that requirement is not subsequently enforceable by one party. *See* Triangle Air Conditioning, Inc. v. Caswell Cnty. Bd. of Educ., 57 N.C. App. 482 (1982) (holding that an oral change order was legally enforceable when both parties, by their conduct, waived a contract requirement that change orders be in writing).

4. Handex of Carolinas, Inc. v. Cnty. of Haywood, 168 N.C. App. 1, 18 (2005).

5. *Brokers*, 33 N.C. App. at 30.

6. Ruby-Collins, Inc. v. City of Charlotte, 740 F. Supp. 1159, 1176 (W.D.N.C. 1990) *aff'd*, 930 F.2d 23 (4th Cir. 1991) ("In a fixed-sum contract, a contractor is not entitled to additional compensation simply because unforeseen difficulties are encountered.").

7. J.R. Graham & Son, Inc. v. Randolph Cnty. Bd. of Ed., 25 N.C. App. 163, 166 (1975).

8. Davidson & Jones, Inc. v. N.C. Dep't of Admin., 315 N.C. 144, 153 (1985).

5.4. What if more funds become available for a project? Can a change order be used to have the contractor already on site perform additional work?

Change orders may be used to authorize additional work only if that work was originally provided for in the project specifications and the contract. The availability of additional funds does not provide justification to expand the scope of the project. For example, if a paving contractor bid on and is awarded a contract to repave five streets and funds subsequently become available to pave two additional streets, a change order cannot be used to expand the scope of the original project to add the two additional streets to the existing contract. If the additional work is subject to competitive bidding requirements, the local government must follow those requirements in contracting for the repaving of the two additional streets.

5.5. Is there a limit on the dollar amount of a change order?

No. A local government clearly is allowed to modify a project in response to changed conditions. However, while the statute does not place a threshold, percent of contract amount, or dollar limit on change orders, fundamental redesign resulting in a project that deviates substantially from the original specifications is not within the scope of the change order exception.

5.6. Do change orders affect the coverage of the contractor's performance and payment bonds?

Change orders need not be approved by the surety company or companies providing performance and payment bonds for the project. Under the terms of the standard performance and payment bonds set out in G.S. 44A-33, the surety company waives its right to be notified of changes and the amount of the bonds will automatically increase to cover a change order that increases the total cost of the contract. (See section II.H.2 of Chapter 2 for further discussion of performance and payment bonds.)

If a change order involves a substantial modification in the plans, it may nevertheless be wise to notify the surety in advance. On rare occasions the surety company might assert that a modification involves such a fundamental alteration of its risk or obligation that the change is not covered by the bond. Of course, if the modification is so drastic as to trigger this concern on the part of the surety, it is likely that use of a change order is inappropriate and that rebidding may be required.

5.7. Must the bidder who was awarded the original contract also perform the change order work?

The answer to this question probably depends on what the contract says or, if it is silent, on what seems reasonable under the circumstances. If the original contractor cannot perform the work specified in the change order or if another source can do the work for less money, then hiring a different firm to do the change order work makes sense. The authorization in G.S. 143-129(e)(4) to undertake additional work without further bidding does not specify that the bidder who was awarded the original contract must be awarded the change order work. In addition, that statute's exemption of change orders from the bidding and other requirements of G.S. Chapter 143, Article 8, would seem to apply regardless of what contractor performs the change order work.

However, if another contractor is awarded additional work under a change order, performance and payment bond requirements will apply if the cost of the project exceeds $300,000 and the contract amount exceeds $50,000. In this case, the local government should require the new contractor to post its own 100 percent performance and payment bonds. The surety company for the original contractor is not required to guarantee the performance of a different contractor, since it has no contractual relationship with that entity. (See section II.H.2 of Chapter 2 for further discussion of performance and payment bonds.)

II. Use of Own Forces

Local governments need not comply with the formal and informal bidding requirements when they undertake construction or repair work with their own personnel, if the work meets certain requirements set out in G.S. 143-135. Under this exception, a local government may use its own employees or officers to perform construction or repair work that the local government would otherwise need to accomplish by following formal or informal competitive bidding procedures to hire a contractor.

5.8. What are the requirements for using our own forces (employees) for construction or repair work?

G.S. 143-135 establishes specific criteria for when a local government may use its own employees for construction or repair work that otherwise would be subject to competitive bidding requirements.

1. The work (*all* of the work) must be performed "by duly elected officers or agents using force account qualified labor on the *permanent* payroll of the agency concerned"—that is, by permanent local government employees or the local government's elected officers.
2. The cost of the work cannot exceed one of the two dollar-threshold limitations. Force account labor may be used if the total cost of the labor on the project does not exceed $50,000, regardless of the cost of other parts of the project, or if the total cost of the project—including all direct and indirect costs of labor, services, materials, supplies, and equipment—does not exceed $125,000. (Under the second standard, labor expenses may exceed $50,000 as long as the total project cost does not exceed $125,000.)
3. The force account work is subject to the approval of the "responsible commission, council, or board" of the local government. Thus, governing board approval is required.
4. Complete and accurate records of the "entire cost" of the work must be maintained by the responsible body for public inspection.

5.9. Can temporary employees perform work under this exception?

No. The force account exception requires the work to be performed by employees on the local government's permanent payroll or its duly elected officers.

5.10. What are the dollar thresholds?

Force account labor may be used when the cost of the project does not exceed one of the two dollar-threshold limitations in the statute:

1. The total cost of the project, including all direct and indirect costs of labor, services, materials, supplies, and equipment, does not exceed $125,000 *or*
2. The total cost of the labor on the project does not exceed $50,000, regardless of the cost of materials, supplies, and equipment.

Note that the project is eligible under the force account exception if *either* dollar threshold is met. For example, if the total labor cost is $35,000 and the materials cost $100,000, the project is eligible even though its total cost exceeds $125,000. Similarly, if the labor cost is $75,000 but the total cost of the project is $110,000, the project is eligible even though the labor cost exceeds $50,000 because the total project cost is less than $125,000.

5.11. Can we divide a project into parts so that we can use our own forces to complete some of the work?

Local governments may not divide up work in order to make a project come in below the dollar limits of G.S. 143-135 and thereby avoid competitive bidding requirements. For example, a local government may not split a $200,000 project with labor costs in excess of $100,000, for which competitive bidding is required, into two $100,000 projects so that the work may be performed by the local government's own forces. However, if the local government has a legitimate basis upon which to divide up the project, such as cash flow or phased funding, it may do so, and if any of the divided components of the project meet either of the dollar-thresholds for the force account exception, the local government may use its own forces to perform the work.

5.12. Does the force account exception apply to materials or supplies purchased for the project?

No. A local government that uses its own forces for construction or repair work must still comply with competitive bidding requirements in purchasing apparatus, supplies, materials, and equipment to be used as part of the project.

5.13. Must one of our employees be a licensed general contractor?

No. Although state law requires a licensed general contractor to supervise any project involving "the construction of any building, highway, public utilities, grading or any improvement or structure,"[9] this requirement does not apply to force account labor. However, the local government must file an owner-builder affidavit with the local building inspector if the project involves construction or repair of a building. See section IX.A of Chapter 3 for further discussion of the owner-contractor affidavit requirement.

III. Emergencies

A construction or repair contract that would otherwise be covered by the formal or informal bidding procedure may be awarded without complying with the statute "in cases of special emergency involving the health and safety of the people or their property."[10]

5.14. What is an "emergency"?

The broad language of the exception would seem to cover all manner of calamities that a local government may face. However, in the case of *Raynor v. Commissioners for the Town of Louisburg*, the North Carolina Supreme Court has interpreted the emergency exception to state competitive bidding laws narrowly, thus limiting its application even in situations involving natural or man-made disasters for which a local government has declared a state of emergency.[11] Discussing the meaning of "emergency" in the competitive bidding context, the court recognized that the determination that an emergency exists is, to some extent, fact-specific. Nonetheless, the court stated that "the emergency . . . must be present, immediate, and existing, and not a condition which may or may not arise in the future or one that is about to arise or may be expected to arise."[12] Thus, a local governing board's factual determination that an emergency exists is subject to judicial review.[13]

In *Raynor*, the court found that the Louisburg town commissioners' concern that the diesel engines at the town's power plant might soon fail due to poor maintenance was not a sufficient emergency to justify bypassing normal competitive bidding procedures in purchasing new engines. Because the town commissioners did not follow the competitive bidding rules, the contract to buy the new engines was void.[14] The court noted that bids for the engines could have been advertised for just one week with replacement ensuing soon thereafter, which suggests that if competitive bidding requirements can be followed without causing harm to public health and safety (or if that harm can be temporarily mitigated), the emergency exception cannot be used.

For example, if a town's water and sewer system suffered damage due to an unforeseen explosion that rendered the system totally inoperable, that situation would likely constitute an emergency for which the town could avoid state competitive bidding requirements to undertake immediate emergency repairs.

However, even in the event of an unforeseen emergency, if the threat to public health and safety can be temporarily mitigated, or if complying with competitive bidding requirements (such as the seven-day advertising requirement for formal contracts and the solicitation of quotes for informal contracts) can be followed without further exacerbating the threat to public health and safety, the emergency exception would not apply. Similarly, anticipating water and sewer system failure in the near future due to neglected maintenance would not constitute an emergency. In fact, this was the situation in the *Raynor* case, and the court specifically noted that local governments cannot take advantage of the emergency exception where the potential emergency has been caused by the local government's own delay in taking action that was foreseeable.

---

9. G.S. 87-1.
10. G.S. 143-129(e)(2).
11. 220 N.C. 348 (1941).
12. *Id.* at 353.
13. *See id.* at 352.
14. *Id.* at 353–54.

5.15. Must the local government declare a state of emergency?

No. The emergency exception to competitive bidding requirements does not trigger the need for the local government to formally declare that a state of emergency exists.[15] However, as discussed in question 5.14 above, the emergency must be "present, immediate, and existing." It is recommended that a local government document the facts of the situation constituting the emergency. If the local government's failure to follow state competitive bidding requirements is challenged, the burden of proof would be on the unit of government to demonstrate that a justification for using the emergency exception existed. Although the court in *Raynor* stated that such facts (including a formal declaration adopted by the governing board) would not be binding on a court, it does provide evidence of the circumstances that the local government determined warranted use of the emergency exception.

5.16. Is governing board approval required?

No. The emergency exception does not require governing board approval of the determination that an emergency exists or of the contract entered into under the exception.

5.17. Is the emergency exception recognized under federal law, such as for FEMA reimbursement in a major disaster?

Most likely not. It is important to note that, even if the emergency exception to state competitive bidding requirements applies, federal regulations may require some form of competition in awarding a contract, even in disaster situations. For example, federal public assistance funding made available to local governments under a presidential disaster declaration is subject to the requirements of the federal Grants Management Common Rule (GMCR). The GMCR requires competitive procurement for most purchase and construction contracts as well as some service contracts.[16] Although an exception is allowed when a "public exigency or emergency . . . will not permit a delay,"[17] local governments should exercise caution in avoiding competitive procurement entirely because a violation of GMCR requirements could result in denial of reimbursement from FEMA for disaster-related expenses, such as debris removal. To the extent feasible, local governments should pre-position competitively bid contracts for goods and services that it anticipates needing during a disaster event, such as debris hauling and emergency supplies. Having pre-positioned competitively bid contracts in place will not only expedite disaster recovery by having contractors ready to mobilize immediately after a disaster event, but it also will avoid potential FEMA reimbursement issues by satisfying the GMCR competitive procurement requirements.

IV. Solid Waste and Sludge Management Facilities

The statutes contain a special procedure for awarding contracts for solid waste management facilities and for the management of sludge generated by water and wastewater treatment facilities.[18] The special rules recognize that

> in some instances it may be beneficial to a unit of local government to award a contract [for such facilities] on the basis of factors other than cost alone, including but not limited to facility design, operational experience, system reliability, energy production efficiency, long-term operational costs, compatibility with source separation and other recycling systems, environmental impact and operational guarantees.[19]

G.S. 143-129.2 establishes criteria that local governments may use as an alternative to the standard competitive bidding rules and procedures in awarding contracts for these types of facilities. In lieu of competitive bidding, a local government may use a competitive request for proposals (RFP) process. Under this alternative RFP process, the local

---

15. Procedures for declaring a local state of emergency are provided under G.S. 166A-19.22.

16. Procurement, 44 C.F.R. § 13.36 (2011) (applicable to federal public assistance funds under a presidentially declared disaster; similar procurement requirements apply to a number of other categories of federal grant funds).

17. 44 C.F.R. § 13.36(d)(4)(i)(B).

18. G.S. 143-129.2.

19. G.S. 143-129.2(b).

government requests certain information from potential respondents that is prescribed by the statute, evaluates proposals received based on statutory standards, and may award the contract to any responsible respondent that the local government determines has submitted the most responsive proposal (a standard of award that is different from the lowest responsive, responsible bidder standard required under competitive bidding procedures). Finally, the statute sets out rules for negotiating with proposers and lists special provisions that the contract between the local government and the person or firm that provides the solid waste or sludge management facility may contain.

The alternative RFP process applies only to the solid waste or sludge management facility itself. Traditional competitive bidding procedures must be followed for facilities and structures that are "ancillary" to a solid waste or sludge management facility and that do not involve "storage and processing of solid waste or sludge or the separation, extraction, and recovery of useful or marketable forms of energy and materials from solid waste at a solid waste management facility." Examples of ancillary facilities include roads, water and sewer lines to the facility limits, transfer stations, scale houses, administration buildings, and residue and bypass disposal sites.[20]

V. Guaranteed Energy Savings Contracts (GESC)

Local governments are authorized to use a modified qualifications-based selection process to enter into contracts for energy-saving improvements to existing buildings or utility systems in which the contractor guarantees that the savings will, over the period of the contract, pay for the cost of the improvements.[21] The law defines the types of energy savings that are to be counted and specifies that they are to be compared with a baseline of previous costs developed by the governmental unit. Such "guaranteed energy savings contracts" (GESCs) are subject to special requirements concerning requests for proposals, award standards, and contract terms.

GESCs are exempt from the normal statutory bidding requirement that apply to construction, repair, or purchase contracts, except for those relating to minority business participation and alternative dispute resolution. Specifically, the minority business requirements of G.S. 143-128.2, -128.3, and -131(b) discussed in Chapter 4 continue to apply to GESCs for work on buildings; the alternative dispute resolution requirements of G.S. 143-128(f1) discussed in section IV of Chapter 3 apply to any such contracts where more than $15,000 is in controversy (the public body may set this figure lower).

As noted above, the energy conservation measures to be installed under the contract must be for an existing building or utility system. They may provide anticipated energy savings or capture lost revenues. The measures may involve alterations and services related to the operation of a facility or a meter, such as the addition of insulation and the installation of storm windows; automatic energy control systems; various types of meters and other equipment to conserve or recycle water and wastewater; other energy conservation measures that conserve energy, water, or other utilities; and training related to the facility's or the meter's operation.[22] The measures may be financed through installment- or lease-purchase agreements.[23]

To enter into a GESC, the local government must issue an RFP, conduct a mandatory pre-bid meeting, have a qualified architect or engineer evaluate the proposals, rank the proposals, obtain cost-savings comparisons from the highest ranked respondent, negotiate price and other contract terms with the highest ranked respondent, and then award the contract. If negotiations with the highest ranked respondent are not successful, the local government may initiate negotiations with the second-highest ranked respondent, and so forth. In making the contract award, the local government must find that the energy savings from the performance of the contract equal or exceed

---

20. G.S. 143-129.2(f).

21. G.S. Chapter 143, Article 3B, Part 2, and G.S. 143-129(e)(8). For more information on the GESC contracting process see "Guaranteed Energy Savings Contracts: Step-By-Step Contracting Process," www.ncpurchasing.unc.edu (click the link to "Tools").

22. G.S. 143-64.17(1).

23. *See* G.S. 160A-20 & -19 and G.S. Chapter 159, Article 8.

the contract's "total cost." The State Energy Office must review the proposed contract before it is awarded. Local Government Commission approval is required if the contract involves financing. Only contractors who have been prequalified by the State Energy Office are considered qualified providers able to bid on local government projects.

The qualified provider to whom the GESC is awarded must provide a bond in the amount of 100 percent of the total savings guaranteed over the term of the contract (GESCs may be for a term of up to twenty years). The purpose of the bond is to guarantee the amount of energy and operational savings promised by the qualified provider under the GESC. The provider must conduct an annual reconciliation comparing the amount of savings guaranteed under the contract to actual savings for the previous twelve months. In the event of a shortfall, the qualified provider pays the difference to the local government. In the event of a surplus, the local government retains the surplus, but that surplus cannot be carried forward to another year.

VI. Airport Construction

Cities and counties may utilize a limited exception to the competitive bidding laws for federally financed construction of airport facilities.[24] Generally, cities and counties must follow state competitive bidding requirements for contracts involving the "acquisition, construction, enlargement, improvement, maintenance, equipment, or operation of airports or other air navigation facilities."[25] But if an airport project is partly or entirely paid for with federal funds, the city or county may follow federal procurement guidelines instead of state bidding requirements.

VII. Other Competitive Bidding Exceptions

The competitive bidding statutes contain a number of other exceptions to bidding requirements for purchase contracts (meaning the purchase of apparatus, supplies, materials, and equipment). Unless the language of the statute specifies that the exception applies to contracts for construction or repair work, the exception is not available for these types of contracts.

5.18. Does the sole source exception apply to contracts for construction or repair work?

No. The sole source exception applies only to purchase contracts. However, the local government may choose to use the sole source exception to purchase materials or equipment related to a construction or repair project if the exception applies to that purchase.

5.19. Does the piggyback exception apply to contracts for construction or repair work?

No. As with the sole source exception, the piggyback exception applies only to purchase contracts. However, the local government may choose to use the piggyback exception to purchase materials or equipment related to a construction or repair project if the exception applies to that purchase. The local government cannot use the piggyback exception to contract with a contractor who is under or has had a contract with another unit of local government to perform construction or repair work.

5.20. Does the group purchasing program exception apply to contracts for construction or repair work?

No. As with the sole source and piggyback exceptions, the group purchasing program exception (sometimes referred to as cooperative purchasing) applies only to purchase contracts. However, the local government may choose to use the group purchasing exception to purchase materials or equipment related to a construction or repair project if the exception applies to that purchase. Local governments should carefully review the group purchasing contract to ensure that the contract does not include labor that constitutes construction or repair work as

---

24. G.S. 63-54(c) (for cities) & -57 (for counties).
25. G.S. 63-54(c).

part of the purchase of the materials. For example, some national group purchasing programs offer contracts for roofing materials that include installation. While the purchase of the roofing materials may be eligible under the group purchasing exception, the installation work constitutes construction and cannot be included in the purchase contract. The local government must follow state competitive bidding procedures to contract for the installation.

The chart in Appendix 5A outlines the exceptions to competitive bidding requirements and indicates which are available for construction and repair contracts.

Appendix 5A Exceptions to Competitive Bidding Requirements

Exception	Applies To	Description	Board Approval Required?	Other Requirements
		Purchases		
Purchase from other units of Government G.S. 143-129(e)(1)	Informal and formal purchases and leases	Purchase directly from another unit of federal, state, or local government anywhere in the U.S.	No	None
Emergency G.S. 143-129(e)(2)	Informal and formal purchases and construction/repair	Present, immediate, and existing special emergency involving public health and safety of people or property	No	None
Fuel Purchase G.S. 143-129(e)(5)	Informal and formal purchases	Purchase of gasoline, diesel fuel, alcohol fuel, motor oil, fuel oil, or natural gas	Informal bidding requirements apply to purchases costing $30,000 or more (including purchases over $90,000)	Informal bidding requirements apply to purchases costing $30,000 or more (including purchases over $90,000)
Sole Source G.S. 143-129(e)(6)	Informal and formal purchases	Available when (1) performance or price competition is not available, (2) product is available from only one source, or (3) standardization or compatibility is the overriding consideration	Yes	None
Group Purchasing Program G.S. 143-129(e)(3)	Informal and formal purchases	Competitive bidding process by a formally organized program offering discount prices to at least two public agencies	No	None
State Contract G.S. 143-129(e)(9)	Informal and formal purchases	Purchases from contracts established by State of N.C. if the contractor is willing to extend the same or more favorable prices, terms, and conditions	No	None
Federal Contract G.S. 143-129(e)(9a)	Informal and formal purchases	Purchases from contracts established by a federal agency if the contractor is willing to extend the same or more favorable prices, terms, and conditions	No	None
Used Goods G.S. 143-129(e)(10)	Informal and formal purchases	Purchase of used goods from a public or private entity; remanufactured, refabricated, or demo goods are not included under this exception	No	None

Appendix 5A Exceptions to Competitive Bidding Requirements (*continued*)

Piggyback G.S. 143-129(g)	Formal purchases	Purchases from contracts entered into by any federal, state, or local government in the U.S. that have been competitively bid within the previous twelve months if the contractor is willing to extend the same or more favorable prices, terms, and conditions	Yes	Board approval at a regular meeting after at least ten days' public notice (notice may be given by publication and electronic means; notice by electronic means only requires governing board approval)
Trade-In G.S. 143-129.7	Informal and formal purchases	Units may include trade-in of used items as part of the specifications for purchases and may award one contract for both the sale of the trade-in item and the purchase of the new item	No	Items sold as a trade-in under G.S. 143-129.7 are not subject to property disposal requirements of Article 12 of Chapter 160A
Transportation Authority Purchases G.S. 143-129(h)	Informal and formal purchases and leases	Regional public transportation authorities (RPTA) and regional transportation authorities (RTA) may use RFP process for purchases	Yes	RFP process required by G.S. 143-129(h); governing board must approve use of RFP process at a regularly scheduled meeting before RFP is issued; governing board must certify that RFP process has been followed and approve contract at a regularly scheduled meeting
Nonprofit Work Centers for Blind and Severely Disabled G.S. 143-129.5	Informal and formal purchases	Purchases from a nonprofit work center for the blind and severely disabled as defined in G.S. 148-48	No	None
School Food Services G.S. 115C-264	Informal and formal purchases	Local school unit purchase of supplies and food for food services (nutrition programs) at school	No	None; federal requirements will apply to food services that are federally funded
School Books G.S. 115C-522(a)	Informal and formal purchases	Local school unit purchase of published books, manuscripts, pamphlets, and periodicals	No	None
		Construction and Repair		
Change Order G.S. 143-129(e)(4)	Informal and formal construction/repair	Construction/repair work undertaken during the progress of a competitively bid project that is within the scope of the original project	No	None

Appendix 5A Exceptions to Competitive Bidding Requirements (*continued*)

Emergency G.S. 143-129(e)(2)	Informal and formal purchases and construction/repair	Present, immediate, and existing special emergency involving public health and safety of people or property	No	None; FEMA procurement requirements will apply in presidentially declared disasters
Force Account Work G.S. 143-135	Construction/repair (within dollar limits)	Use of unit's own employees (on permanent payroll) and officers to perform construction work when either (1) total cost of the project is under $125,000 or (2) total cost of labor is under $50,000	Yes	Purchases of materials used on the project still subject to competitive bidding requirements; unit must keep accurate records of entire cost of project
Guaranteed Energy Savings Contract (GESC) G.S. 143-129(e)(8)	Informal and formal construction/repair and related purchases	GESC for improvements to existing facilities to achieve energy savings sufficient to pay for the costs of the improvements over the term of the contract	Yes, if financing of project subject to LGC approval	RFP process required under Article 3B of Chapter 143
Construction Management at-Risk (CM@R) G.S. 143-129(e)(11)	Informal and formal construction and repair	Construction or repair projects performed by a construction manager at-risk	No	CM@R hired under the Mini-Brooks Act QBS process (G.S. 143-64.31); contracts for construction project subject to requirements of G.S. 143-128.1
Solid Waste Management Facilities G.S. 143-129.2	Construction and operation of solid waste management facilities	Contract for design, construction, operation, management and maintenance of highly complex and innovative solid waste management facilities and sludge management facilities; "ancillary facilities" (water and sewer lines and transfer stations) are excluded from the exemption	No	RFP process is optional; if not used, construction or repair work is subject to competitive bidding
		Information Technology Goods and Services		
State ITS G.S. 143-129(e)(7)	Informal and formal purchases of information technology goods and services	Purchases made through contracts established by the State Office of Information Technology Services ("information technology" defined under G.S. 147-33.81(2))	No	None
IT Goods and Services G.S. 143-129.8	Informal and formal purchases of information technology goods and services	Contract for combination of information technology goods and services ("information technology" defined under G.S. 147-33.81(2))	No	RFP process required under G.S. 143-129.8

Chapter 6

Post-Award Payments to Contractors, Disputes, and Claims

Chapter 6

Post-Award Payments to Contractors, Disputes, and Claims

I. Introduction

After the local government awards the construction contract(s) and the construction or repair work commences, disputes and claims may arise during the course of the project. While many of these issues are governed by the terms and conditions of the contract and the law that surrounds construction contract disputes, several statutes are applicable to particular situations involving contracts with public entities. These situations, discussed in this chapter, include retainage of payments due to contractors, performance and payment bond claims, liens, and dispute resolution procedures.

II. Payments Due to Contractors; Retainage

Contractors on public construction projects are entitled to be paid on a timely basis, and the local government is entitled to performance under the contract. These two interests sometimes collide when the contractor demands payment and the local government is of the opinion that the contractor has not fully performed. Section 143-134.1 of the North Carolina General Statutes (hereinafter G.S.) governs when the contractor must be paid as well as when a local government may withhold payment and for what reasons.

6.1. When must contractors be paid?

G.S. 143-134.1 does not specify a time frame within which contractors are to receive periodic payments during the course of the contract (sometimes referred to as "progress payments"). In fact, the statute does not even appear to require that periodic payments be made at all, though, practically speaking, periodic payments are customary on construction projects if for no other reason than to enable the prime contractor to pay his or her employees, subcontractors, and materials suppliers. Thus, periodic payments, while not specifically required by statute, are typically provided for under the contract, and disputes arising from periodic payments will be decided by the terms and conditions of the contract and case law. Assuming periodic payments are provided for under the contract, withholding sums from period payments will be governed by state law (see discussions below on retainage).

G.S. 143-134.1(a) does require a local government to pay the balance due (i.e., the final payment) to prime contractors within forty-five days after the project has been accepted by the local government, certified as complete by the architect or engineer, or occupied and used by the local government, whichever happens first. This requirement is consistent with that of G.S. 133-1.1(f), which prohibits final payment to contractors and designers until a certificate of compliance has been issued (see section IX.C of Chapter 3 for a discussion of certificates of compliance).

6.2. What happens if the local government makes a late payment to a contractor?

If the local government does not make final payment to the prime contractor within the forty-five day period described above, the contractor is to be paid interest on the unpaid balance starting on the forty-sixth day and continuing to accrue until payment is made. The interest rate is 1 percent per month or a fraction thereof unless a lower rate is agreed on. The same interest penalty applies if the local government is late in making a periodic payment. In addition, the local government cannot delay paying one prime contractor merely because another prime contractor has not completed his or her contract (general, electrical, plumbing, and heating and air conditioning contractors may all be "prime contractors," if the separate-prime contracting system is used).

6.3. What if the final payment is late because the contractor delayed completing the project?

In this instance, if the architect or engineer determines that the delay in completing the project was caused by the contractor, the local government may assume occupancy and use of the project and will not be obligated to pay the contractor interest on any amount of payment withheld beyond forty-five days. This is also the case if the local government withholds a reasonable sum from the final payment to ensure correction of any final items or conditions on the project (the "punch list"); interest is not owed to the contract on sums withheld from the final payment for this reason.

6.4. What rules apply to a contractor's payments to subcontractors?

Prime contractors are generally required to pay subcontractors within seven days after receipt of each periodic or final payment to the contractor from the local government. Payments to subcontractors are to be based on work completed or service called for under the subcontract. Past-due payments to subcontractors also accrue interest, beginning on the eighth day, at the rate of 1 percent per month or a fraction thereof on whatever unpaid balance may be due.[1]

Despite this general requirement, prime contractors are permitted, when they make application and certification to the owner for payment, to withhold application and certification for payment to subcontractors for the reasons listed below:

1. unsatisfactory job progress;
2. defective condition not remedied;
3. disputed work;
4. third-party claims;
5. failure of the subcontractor to make timely payments for labor, equipment, and materials;
6. damage to the prime contractor or another subcontractor; and
7. reasonable evidence that the subcontract cannot be completed for the balance of the subcontract sum.[2]

Prime contractors may also withhold application and certification for payment of a reasonable amount for retainage. A prime contractor's percentage of retainage on payments to a subcontractor may not exceed the percentage of retainage on payments made by the owner to the prime contractor. In other words, if the local government retains a certain percentage of payment to the prime contractor (see discussion of retainage below), the prime contractor may withhold that same percentage from payments to subcontractors. The prime contractor must pay the subcontractor 1 percent interest per month or a fraction thereof on any excess retainage.[3]

6.5. What is retainage?

Retainage is the amount of payment the local government withholds ("retains") from the prime contractor (or contractors in the case of separate-prime contracting) until the construction project has been satisfactorily completed. Sometimes retainage is held until the end of the project to ensure completion of those last remaining

---

1. Section 143-134.1(b) of the North Carolina General Statutes (hereinafter G.S.).
2. G.S. 143-134.1(d).
3. G.S. 143-134.1(c).

items identified by the local government (the "punch list"). In other instances, retainage is held because of poor or unsatisfactory performance during the course of the project.

6.6. Under what circumstances is retainage allowed?

Retainage is *not allowed* on projects costing less than $100,000. For projects costing $100,000 or more, retainage may be withheld from periodic and final payments, but the amount retained may not exceed 5 percent of the payment amount. In addition, specific limitations on retainage apply at various points during the construction project.[4]

1. Until the project is 50 percent complete, the local government cannot retain more than 5 percent of any periodic payment owed to the prime contractor.
2. When the project is 50 percent complete, no further retainage is allowed as long as the contractor's performance is satisfactory. To stop retainage under these circumstances, the local government must have the written consent of the surety.
3. When a certificate of substantial completion is issued or upon beneficial occupancy, all remaining retainage must be released, though the local government may retain up to two-and-a-half times the value of any remaining work to secure completion or correction of that work (the "punch list" work).[5]
4. "Line-item" release of retained funds is required for "early finishing trades" (subcontractors who complete 100 percent of their work before the project is 50 percent complete, including structural steel, piling, caisson, and demolition[6]).

In addition to these requirements, local governments may also withhold additional amounts from payments to the contractor for unsatisfactory performance, defective workmanship not remedied, disputed work, or third-party claims filed against the local governments.[7] While this additional retainage authorization is not capped at 5 percent of the remaining periodic or final payments, a local government should not retain more than it can document is necessary to remedy the situation for which the funds are withheld.

6.7. Is interest charged on retainage?

No interest is charged on retainage, only on late payments.[8]

6.8. If the local government releases retainage and pays the contractor, does that payment void any warranties on the project?

Release of retainage does not affect any applicable warranties on work done by the prime contractor or subcontractors.[9]

6.9. What if the project is funded with federal grant funds that impose different requirements or limitations on retainage?

The retainage statute specifically provides that the terms and conditions of federal grant funds preempt state retainage rules if state law conflicts with federal regulations.[10] In such situations, the local government must specify federal preemption of the state retainage statute in its bid documents.

---

4. G.S. 143-134.1(b1).
5. G.S. 143-134.1(b3).
6. G.S. 143-134.1(b2).
7. G.S. 143-134.1(e).
8. *See* RPR & Assocs., Inc. v. Univ. of N.C.-Chapel Hill, 153 N.C. App. 342, 351 (2002).
9. G.S. 143-134.1(b4).
10. G.S. 143-134.1(b6).

III. Dispute Resolution Requirement for Building Projects

As discussed in section IV of Chapter 3, all local governments must provide a dispute resolution process for nearly all *building* erection, construction, alteration, and repair *projects, even those that are not subject to any competitive bidding requirements.*[11] The local government may impose a minimum "amount in controversy" threshold of up to $15,000 before requiring parties to participate in the dispute resolution process. Note that the dispute resolution process requirement applies *only* to building projects; local governments may, however, choose to provide this process on non-building construction projects.

6.10. What must be provided for in the dispute resolution process?

The governmental unit has two options in fulfilling the dispute resolution requirement. It may use the dispute resolution process adopted by the State Building Commission pursuant to G.S. 143-135.26(12),[12] or it may design its own alternative process. The local government's dispute resolution process must comply with the following statutory requirements:[13]

1. The process must include mediation (the state's process includes mediation as well).
2. The process must be made available to all parties involved in the project for any issues arising out of the contract or construction process, including designers, contractors, subcontractors, and the local government itself (the dispute resolution process does not apply to disappointed bidders).

In addition, the local government may include the following provisions in its dispute resolution process:

1. Set a reasonable threshold on the amount in controversy that must be involved before one party may require others to participate in the dispute resolution process, thus avoiding the process being used to resolve nominal disputes. The threshold may not exceed $15,000.
2. Require that the costs of the dispute resolution process be divided between or among the parties to the dispute. If the governmental unit is one of the parties, it must pay at least one-third of the cost.
3. Require a party to participate in mediation concerning a dispute as a precondition to initiating litigation about the dispute (if the local government opts to impose this requirement, the requirement must be included in the construction contract).

6.11. What if the dispute resolution requirement differs from typical (or boilerplate) contract provisions?

The dispute resolution method mandated by statute differs from the typical contractual arrangement under standard American Institute of Architect (AIA) documents, where all disputes first go to the architect for decision. Because state law preempts contract language, the local government must modify the language of the contract. While the local government could still require that disputes be reviewed initially by the architect, the dispute resolution statute mandates that all parties to the dispute be able to use the dispute resolution process.

Note that the statutory rules also require modifying another provision of the standard AIA contract. In cases where the dispute moves beyond the architect for resolution, the standard AIA contract contemplates relying on the independent decision of one or more arbitrators. This of course is contrary to mediation, where the parties attempt to resolve their own problem with the help of a mediator.

---

11. G.S. 143-128(g). Building construction and repair projects costing less than $30,000 are not subject to state competitive bidding requirements.

12. N.C. ADMIN. CODE tit. 1, ch. 30H, http://reports.oah.state.nc.us/ncac/title%2001%20-%20administration/chapter%20 30%20-%20state%20construction/subchapter%20h/subchapter%20h%20rules.html. Examples of local government dispute resolution policies are available on the School of Government's local government purchasing and contracting website, www.sog.unc.edu/node/770.

13. G.S. 143-128(f1).

6.12. What other options are available to resolve contract disputes?

Except for the mandated procedures in G.S. 143-128(f1), the options available for resolving conflicts in local government construction contracts are similar in many ways to those for settling disagreements in construction contracts that involve only private parties. Lawsuits may be filed, settlements may be reached, or—if the contract so provides or the parties agree to do so—other alternative dispute resolution methods, such as arbitration, may be used. Of course, to the extent that a mandatory, binding arbitration provision is incompatible with the legal requirements of G.S. 143-128(f1), it would not be enforceable against a local government. Governments do not have legal authority to agree to unlawful contract terms.

IV. Liens

In the private sector, disputes regarding nonpayment of contractors, subcontractors, and suppliers are sometimes resolved by filing liens against the project itself. G.S. Chapter 44A, Articles 1 and 2, provide for personal and real property liens as remedies for unpaid contractors on private projects. These lien statutes are not applicable to public construction or repair projects.

6.13. Can a contractor or subcontractor file a lien against public property?

The lien statutes set out in G.S. Chapter 44A, Articles 1 and 2, do not apply to the contracts or property of local governments (including local government funds, which are a form of property). Except in very limited cases (see, for example, G.S. 160A-20), North Carolina law does not permit or recognize the encumbering of public property with liens, mortgages, or other types of security interests, including in the context of a construction project payment dispute. Instead, to ensure that subcontractors and suppliers are paid by the prime contractor on a public project, Article 3 of G.S. Chapter 44A requires the prime contractor to provide payment bonds of 100 percent of all contracts costing more than $50,000 on projects costing more than $300,000[14] (see section II.H.2 of Chapter 2 for further discussion of payment bonds). North Carolina courts have long-viewed the bond provisions of G.S. Chapter 44A, Article 3, as taking the place of statutory mechanics' liens where public contracts are involved.[15] As Justice William B. Rodman Jr. wrote in *American Bridge Division United States Steel Corp. v. Brinkley*,[16]

> Our Constitution contains a mandate directing the General Assembly to enact legislation to give mechanics and laborers a lien on the subject matter of their labor. N. C. Constitution, Art. XIV, sec. 4 [now Article X, Section 3]. Public policy prohibits the acquisition of liens for labor or materials used or furnished in the construction of a public edifice or way. Noland Co. v. Trustees, 190 N.C. 250, 129 S.E. 577, and cases there cited.
>
> The General Assembly has, by the enactment of G.S. 44-14 and G.S. 136-28 [G.S. 44-14 was a predecessor of G.S. Chapter 44A, Article 3], given to laborers and materialmen engaged in public construction a substantial equivalent to the lien given laborers and materialmen engaged in private construction. The surety

---

14. G.S. 44A-26.

15. Snow v. Durham Cnty. Comm'rs, 112 N.C. 335 (1893) (a courthouse cannot be made subject to any lien for labor or materials); Morganton Hardware Co. v. Morganton Graded Sch., 150 N.C. 680 (1909) (public school building is not subject to a statutory lien for materials furnished for its construction); Noland Co. v. Bd. of Trustees of S. Pines Sch., 190 N.C. 250, 252–53 (1925) ("It is the uniform holding that no lien can be secured or enforced against a public building. *Warner v. Hallyburton*, 187 N.C. 414, 121 S.E. 756 (public school building); *Ingold v. Hickory*, 178 N.C. 614, 101 S.E. 525 (public school building); *Scheflow v. Pierce*, 176 N.C. 91, 97 S.E. 167 (sewer system, town of Tarboro); *Hutchinson v. Com'rs*, 172 N.C. 844 (county home); *McCausland v. Const. Co.*, 172 N.C. 708, 90 S.E. 1010 (public school building); *Fore v. Feimster*, 171 N.C. 551, 88 S.E. 977 (county home); *Hdw. Co. v. Graded School*, 150 N.C. 680, 64 S.E. 764; *S. c.*, 151 N.C. 507 (public school building); *Gastonia v. Engineering Co.*, 131 N.C. 359, 42 S.E. 857 (municipal electric-lighting plant and waterworks pumping station); *Snow v. Com'rs.*, 112 N.C. 335 (courthouse).")

16. 255 N.C. 162, 164 (1961).

on the bond is, for practical purposes, the substitute for the lien. *Lumber Co. v. Lawson*, 195 N.C. 840, 143 S.E. 847; *Mfg. Co. v. Blaylock*, 192 N.C. 407, 135 S.E. 136.

Consistent with this line of court decisions, Article 3 itself states that the "addition of this Article [Article 3] shall not be construed as making the provisions of Articles 1 and 2 of Chapter 44A of the General Statutes apply to public bodies or public buildings."[17]

6.14. Since liens against public property are not allowed, what protects the contractor if he or she is not paid by the local government?

While payment bonds protect subcontractors by ensuring a remedy if they are not paid by the prime contractor, there is no similar protection for the contractor in the event of nonpayment by the local government. The contractor may make use of the dispute resolution process discussed in section III of this chapter (if the project involves a public building). If the dispute resolution effort is not successful or not available, the contractor's only course of action is to pursue litigation against the local government.

6.15. What if a contractor or subcontractor attempts to file a lien against a public project?

Any purported mechanics' or materialmens' lien that a contractor or subcontractor attempts to file against a public building or other public property is null and void. Nonetheless, it is in the local government's best interest for its attorney to object as quickly and strongly as possible to the filing of a purported lien, even if the filing is supposedly done out of ignorance of the law. This is especially the case since the clerk of superior court is allowed to accept documents *for filing only* that do not meet the criteria set out in G.S. 44A-12.1(a) for the indexing, docketing, or recording of claims of lien on real property.[18]

As to those criteria, G.S. 44A-12.1(a) specifies that the clerk may not "index, docket, or record a claim of lien on real property or other document purporting to claim or assert a lien on real property in such a way as to affect the title to any real property unless the document [i]s offered for filing under [G.S. Chapter 44A, Article 2] or another statute that provides for indexing and docketing of claims of lien on real property" and "[a]ppears on its face to contain all of the information required by the statute under which it is offered for filing." Presumably a document that on its face states an invalid claim of lien on a public building or other public real property, a claim that purportedly is made under a law that does not apply to public entities (G.S. Chapter 44A, Article 2), does not contain the type of information that is needed for indexing, docketing, and recording a claim of lien. However, there may be some confusion on this point, especially if a document is offered "for filing only."

Confusion may also arise from G.S. 44A-12.1(d), which pertains to the filing of claims of lien by attorneys. That statute requires the clerk not to reject "for indexing, docketing, recording, or filing" any "claim of lien on real property, a claim of lien on real property with a notice of claim of lien upon funds attached thereto, or other document purporting to claim or assert a lien on real property that is filed by an attorney licensed in the State of North Carolina," *if the document "otherwise complies with"* G.S. 44A-12.1(a) (emphasis added). In the case of public entities, of course, the document does not meet the requirements of the statute (see preceding paragraph) and is null and void despite being filed by an attorney.

6.16. Are there any consequences for filing a lien against public property?

G.S. 44A-12.1(c) prohibits filing or attempting to file a lien on real property if the filing is made with the knowledge that the lien is not authorized by statute or is done for an improper purpose "such as to hinder, harass, or otherwise wrongfully interfere with any person." Any person unlawfully filing the lien is subject to criminal prosecution. A violation of this prohibition is punishable as a Class I felony.

---

17. G.S. 44A-34. See James River Equip., Inc. v. Tharpe's Excavating, Inc., 179 N.C. App. 336, 345 (2006) (dismissal of lien claim against local school board affirmed citing G.S. 44A-34).

18. G.S. 44A-12.1(b).

6.17. Must a local government hire a lien agent?

Private construction project owners are required by G.S. 44A-11.1 to hire a lien agent to manage lien claims on the project. Since the lien agent requirement is found in Article 2 of G.S. Chapter 44A (which applies to private entities) and not in Article 3 (which applies to public entities), the lien agent requirement does not apply to local governments. In addition, since the function of the lien agent is to manage lien claims filed against the project owner, a situation that is not statutorily permissible in the case of local governments, there is no need, and arguably, no authorization, for a local government to hire a lien agent.

V. Performance and Payment Bonds in the Claims Process

Performance bonds on the construction and repair contracts of local governments are executed, as noted above in section IV and as discussed in section II.H.2 of Chapter 2, for the protection of the local government that is constructing the project.[19] Payment bonds protect interests that are different from those protected by performance bonds. Although payment bonds are required by and filed with the local government, they are executed to protect those who furnish materials or perform labor for which a contractor, subcontractor, or construction manager at-risk is liable.[20]

The protections under the two forms of bonds are exclusive and require separate actions by the aggrieved party. Local governments seeking performance by the general contractor pursue recovery only under the performance bond, while subcontractors and suppliers seeking payment from the contractor pursue recovery only under the payment bond. Actions on payment bonds may be brought directly by persons who have not been paid for labor or materials they furnished to either the general contractor or a subcontractor for a construction or repair project.[21]

6.18. What is the difference between liability under a bond and an obligation under a contract?

The difference between the surety's liability under these bonds and the local government's obligation to pay under the contract should be kept clear at all times. Each bond—performance and payment—must be for 100 percent of the contract amount, including increases due to approved change orders, and must remain in effect for the life of the project. Furthermore, G.S. 44A-30(a) explicitly forbids the contractor, the surety, and the contracting body from reducing or limiting the contractor's or surety's liability as set out in the bond law, G.S. Chapter 44A, Article 3.[22] The local government is liable only for the amount it originally agreed to pay under the contract, along with any sums added by approved change orders.

6.19. What if a surety wishes to settle a claim for less than its potential financial exposure under a bond?

Occasionally one hears of a surety who wishes to settle a claim with a local government in a manner that reduces the surety's potential financial exposure prior to the project's successful completion and the satisfactory payment of all potential claimants under the payment bond. Engaging in this practice is not simply unwise for the local government. As noted, it is also illegal. The surety must spend whatever it takes, up to 100 percent of the contract amount, including approved change orders (what is called the "face amount" of the bond[23]), to see that the project is satisfactorily completed. The surety must also spend whatever is necessary, up to another such face amount (100 percent of the contract amount, including approved change orders), to see that the subcontractors and materials suppliers are properly paid. On the other hand, the surety is not liable above the face amount of

---

19. G.S. 44A-26(a)(1).
20. G.S. 44A-26(a)(2).
21. G.S. 44A-27.
22. Presumably, this prohibition does not prohibit the parties from agreeing to a settlement of litigation in an amount that is less than the surety's liability.
23. G.S. 44A-29.

each bond. A judgment against a surety may be reduced or set aside if the judgment would cause the face amount to be exceeded.[24]

6.20. At what point should a local government contact a surety if there is a problem with the contractor?

If a contractor does not meet his or her contractual obligations, construction managers and local government attorneys vary in their opinions of the next steps that should be taken. Some suggest that the local government should first work with the contractor, perhaps threatening to contact the surety company, in an effort to improve performance. Others argue for contacting the surety early on in the process, in case alternative arrangements must be made for completion of the work. In any case, bringing in a surety suggests that there is a major problem with the project. The local government should be able to contact the surety easily through the information on the bond provided by the contractor. The local government's attorney also may obtain up-to-date surety contact information, including names and addresses for service of legal process on the surety's registered agent, from the Office of the North Carolina Secretary of State.

6.21. What information related to payment bonds must the contractor provide to his or her subcontractors?

A contractor must provide to each subcontractor he or she hires a "contractor's project statement" that contains the following information:[25]

1. the name of the project;
2. the physical address of the project;
3. the name of the contracting body (the local government);
4. the name of the contractor;
5. the name, phone number, and mailing address of an agent authorized by the contractor to accept service of the requests for payment bond, the notice of public subcontract, and the notice of claim on payment bond referenced in subsection (b) of this section;
6. the name and address of the principal place of business of the surety issuing the payment bond required by G.S. 44A-26(a) for the construction contract.

The contractor's subcontractors are then required to provide the contractor's project statement to each lower tier subcontractor or materials supplier with whom they contract.[26] No agreement between the contractor and a subcontractor (or between a subcontractor and a lower tier subcontractor) is enforceable against the subcontractor (or lower tier subcontractor) until the contractor's project statement has been provided.[27]

6.22. How does the contractor identify the lower tier subcontractors on the project and know when they have (or have not) been paid?

While the contractor will certainly know who his or her direct subcontractors are (these are the subcontractors the general contractor has hired), the contractor may not know whom the various subcontractors have hired (lower tier subcontractors) or from whom the subcontractors have purchased materials. And yet, these lower tier subcontractors and suppliers are entitled to make a claim against the contractor's payment bond for payments owed to them by subcontractors, thus leaving the contractor and his or her surety exposed to liability for nonpayments beyond the contractor's direct control. In addition, a contractor may be exposed to what is referred to as a "double-payment" problem. The double payment occurs when the general contractor pays a subcontractor in full, but that subcontractor fails to pay in full *its* subcontractors or suppliers (or those subcontractors or suppliers fail to pay *their* subcontractor or suppliers and on down the line). The general contractor is then exposed to double payment when the unpaid, lower tier claimants make claims on the general contractor's payment bond. Because these lower tier claimants have 120 days from the date of their last furnishing of labor or materials within which to

---

24. *Id.*
25. G.S. 44A-27(f)(1).
26. G.S. 44A-27(f)(2).
27. G.S. 44A-27(f)(3).

serve their notice of claim on the payment bond (discussed below), the general contractor may not know of these claims until long after its direct subcontractors have been paid.

To avoid the double-payment problem and give the contractor a means by which to identify lower tier subcontractors and suppliers who might be in a position to make a claim against the payment bond, all subcontractors (except first-tier subcontractors) must serve on the general contractor a notice of public subcontract in the form provided by the statute.[28] This requirement applies to claims against the payment bond in excess of $20,000 that become due more than seventy-five days before the notice of public subcontract is given to the general contractor.

6.23. What are the procedures for actions on payment bonds?

The basic rules for actions by subcontractors or materials suppliers on payment bonds are set out in G.S. 44A-27 and -28. A claimant—defined in G.S. 44A-25(1) to include anyone "entitled to maintain an action on a bond described [in Article 3 of Chapter 44]"[29]—may bring an action on a payment bond in his or her own name when both of the following two conditions have been met:

1. The subcontractor or supplier has performed labor or furnished materials for the construction project as required by any contract for which a payment bond has been given pursuant to the provisions of Article 3.
2. The subcontractor or supplier has not been paid in full within ninety days after the date on which the claimant performed the last of the labor or furnished the last of the materials for which he or she claims payment.[30]

Under these circumstances, the claimant is entitled to prosecute the action (the claim under the payment bond) to final judgment and have execution on the judgment.[31]

If the claimant has no express or implied contractual relationship with the contractor who posted the bond but instead has a "direct contractual relationship" with a subcontractor of that contractor, then the claimant must meet a special notice requirement before bringing an action. He or she must, within 120 days from the date on which the claimant performed the last of the labor or furnished the last of the materials for which payment is sought, give written notice to the contractor who posted the bond.[32] If the claimant does not provide notice within the 120-day period, he or she loses the right to make a claim under the contractor's payment bond. In addition, the claimant may not make a claim for payment due on labor or materials provided more than seventy-five days prior to the date on which the claimant provided its notice of public subcontract to the general contractor.

The claimant's notice to the contractor must state with substantial accuracy the amount claimed and the name of the person for whom the work was performed or to whom the material was furnished. The notice must be served on the contractor by certified mail or by signature confirmation provided by the U.S. Postal Service at any place where the contractor's office is regularly maintained for transacting business, to the contractor's agent who is authorized to accept service of requests for payment bond claims, or "in any manner provided by law for the service of summons."[33]

Within seven calendar days of receiving the claimant's notice, the contractor must send the claimant a copy of the payment bond applicable to the contract under which the claimant is seeking payment. If the general contractor complies with this requirement, the claimant cannot recover for labor or materials it provided more than

---

28. G.S. 44A-27(d).
29. Unlike the federal Miller Act, which Article 3 mirrors, a subcontractor or supplier is not required to have a direct contractual relationship with the general contractor in order to bring a claim under a payment bond. Presumably, any subcontractor or supplier who provides labor or materials on the project is eligible to maintain a claim against a payment bond against the general contractor. *See* HSI N.C., LLC v. Diversified Fire Prot. of Wilmington, Inc., 169 N.C. App. 767 (2005).
30. G.S. 44A-26(a).
31. G.S. 44A-27(a).
32. 44A-27(b).
33. G.S. 44A-27(b), (c).

seventy-five days before the potential claimant served its notice of public subcontract (discussed in question 6.22, above) on the general contractor.

Actions on payment bonds must be brought "in a court of appropriate jurisdiction in a county where the construction contract or any part thereof is to be or has been performed."[34] The action cannot be brought in counties where parts may have been fabricated or services performed if the improvement at issue is not located in or does not span the site of the actual project itself.[35]

Payment bond actions must commence within one year from either the day on which the claimant performed the last of the labor or furnished the last of the material or the day on which final settlement was made with the contractor (i.e., when the contractor received final payment from the local government), whichever is later.[36]

A surety company's total liability for all claims under a payment bond is limited to the face amount of the bond, as noted in question 6.19, above. A judgment against a surety company can be reduced or set aside on the surety's motion if the surety shows that the judgment will cause the face amount of the bond to be exceeded.[37] Also recall, however, that the amount of the 100 percent bond can increase without the surety's knowledge or permission as the size of the project increases (typically through approved change orders). For this reason, many bonds do not actually state a specific face amount but instead reference the project cost.

The local government must furnish, at cost, "upon not less than 10 days' notice and request," a certified copy of the payment bond and the construction contract covered by the bond to anyone entitled to bring an action or to any defendant in any action on a payment bond, and the certified copy is prima facie evidence of the contents, execution, and delivery of the payment bond and construction contract.[38]

6.24. If the general contractor has not paid a subcontractor or supplier, can the local government make that payment and deduct the amount from its payment to the general contractor?

Sometimes a subcontractor or supplier who claims that payment is due from the general contractor will contact the local government directly to request payment. Under no circumstances should the local government make payment to a subcontractor or supplier with whom it does not have a direct contractual relationship. First, the local government has no legal authority to make payment to any individual or business with which it does not have a contract (by definition, subcontractors are not under contract with the local government). Second, the local government's payments to the general contractor are governed under specific statutory requirements that limit when the unit may retain (withhold) payments from the general contractor (see section II of this chapter for further discussion of retainage). Third, the contractor may have a valid reason for withholding payment from the subcontractor, such as in the case of poor performance by the subcontractor. The local government should not insert itself into a payment dispute between a general contractor and a subcontractor. As noted in question 6.23, above, the local government is required to provide a certified copy of the payment bond and construction contract covered by the bond to a claimant. This is the only action the local government should take if contacted by a subcontractor claiming a payment owed by the general contractor.

6.25. What are the procedures for an action by a local government on a performance bond?

It is unclear to what extent the special procedural rules for payment bonds described above also apply to actions on performance bonds brought by local governments. While G.S. 44A-25(1) defines "claimant" to include the "contracting body" (that is, the local government) in a suit to enforce the performance bond, none of the procedural statutes discussed above refer to performance bonds, but only to payment bonds. Given the lack of specific statutory procedures established for performance bond claims, a local government should consult with its attorney before contacting the surety to pursue a performance bond claim.

---

34. G.S. 44A-28(a).
35. McClure Estimating Co. v. H.G. Reynolds Co., Inc., 136 N.C. App. 176 (1999).
36. G.S. 44A-28(b).
37. G.S. 44A-29.
38. G.S. 44A-31.

6.26. Can a successful claimant on a performance or payment bond action recover its attorneys' fees?

In the court's discretion, attorneys' fees may be awarded to the prevailing party in an action based on either a performance or a payment bond if the judge finds that there was an unreasonable refusal by the losing party to fully resolve the matter on which the suit or defense was based. The statute defines "prevailing party" as either a plaintiff who obtains a judgment of at least 50 percent of the amount sought or a defendant who defends a matter resulting in a judgment of less than 50 percent of the amount sought against it.[39]

6.27. What are the procedures for making performance or payment claims if the contractor made deposits in lieu of bonds?

As discussed in section II.H.2 of Chapter 2 (specifically, question 2.76), in lieu of requiring payment and performance bonds, a local government may require the contractor to make a deposit of money, certified check, or government securities for the full amount of the contract "to secure the faithful performance of the terms of [the] contract and the payment of all sums due for labor and materials in a manner consistent with Article 3 of Chapter 4A."[40] If the local government chooses to require a deposit in lieu of bonds, it assumes all the obligations, liabilities, and duties of a surety as provided for under Article 3. However, the statutes are not clear on the procedures to be used for prosecuting a performance or payment claim when deposits in lieu of bonds are required.

For example, as noted earlier in this section (see question 6.23), G.S. 44A-28(b) allows a subcontractor to begin an action on a payment bond at any time within one year from the day on which the last of the labor or material was furnished or final settlement was made with the contractor, whichever is later. Must the local government, because it is regarded as a surety with respect to deposits made with it by a contractor in lieu of providing bonds, retain the full amount of such deposits until the one-year period for actions by subcontractors has expired? A conservative approach would be to answer this question in the affirmative, though such an interpretation delays return of the contractor's deposit. However, if the local government returns the contractor's deposit before the expiration of the one-year period for payment claim actions by subcontractors, it could expose itself to liability for those claims.

39. G.S. 44A-35.
40. G.S. 143-129(c).

Chapter 7

Hiring Architects, Engineers, and Surveyors: Requirements under the Mini-Brooks Act

Chapter 7

Hiring Architects, Engineers, and Surveyors: Requirements under the Mini-Brooks Act

I. Introduction

In North Carolina, the procurement of professional services performed by architects, engineers, surveyors, and alternative construction delivery method firms is governed by Section 143-64.31 of the North Carolina General Statutes (hereinafter G.S.), sometimes referred to as the Mini-Brooks Act after the federal Brooks Act, which state law mirrors. Under the Mini-Brooks Act, local governments select an architect, engineer, or surveyor based primarily on the firm or individual's qualifications, not the cost of the service or fees. This method of procurement is known as qualifications-based selection (QBS), and it differs significantly from the lowest responsive, responsible bidder standard of award for contracts subject to competitive bidding.

This chapter addresses contracting with architects, engineers, and surveyors. A modified form of the Mini-Brooks Act also applies to contracting for alternative construction delivery methods—construction management at-risk, design-build, design-build bridging, and public-private partnerships. See Chapter 3 for a discussion of the contracting requirements for these alternative construction delivery methods.

II. QBS Process Requirements

The QBS process must be used by local government for all contracts involving architectural, engineering, or surveying services, regardless of the cost of the contract.

7.1. What is the QBS process?

The QBS process is a procurement process that focuses on the qualifications of potential firms rather than their fees or the price of the contract. The architect, engineer, or surveyor that the local government wishes to contract with is selected based on "demonstrated competence and qualification for the type of professional services rendered."[1] This is typically done by using a request for qualifications (RFQ) to solicit responses from interested firms and individuals.

7.2. Is QBS the same as competitive bidding?

No. QBS is not competitive bidding, which focuses on price under the lowest responsive, responsible bidder standard of award. In fact, the initial determination of which firm is the best qualified must be done "without regard" to the fee or price other than unit cost (an example of unit cost would be a general hourly fee, but articulation of

1. Section 143-64.31(a) of the North Carolina General Statutes (hereinafter G.S.).

fees that can be easily correlated as a fixed price or bid is prohibited). So the local government cannot request firms to submit an estimated total fee or contract price when they respond to the RFQ.

7.3. What contracts does the QBS process apply to?

The QBS process must be used by local governments when contracting for architectural, engineering, and surveying services as well as for alternative construction delivery methods—construction management at-risk, design-build, design-build bridging, and public-private partnerships (see Chapter 3 for a discussion of alternative construction delivery methods).

7.4. Does the QBS process apply in emergency situations?

No. G.S. 143-64.31 specifically provides that its requirements do not apply "in cases of special emergency involving the health and safety of the people or their property." While the term "special emergency" is not defined, a local government should interpret this term narrowly and use the QBS process only when there is an imminent or actual threat to public health and safety (see section III of Chapter 5 for further discussion of the definition of "emergency"). If the QBS process can be used without exacerbating the threat of harm, the local government should comply with the statutory requirements.

7.5. Is there a minimum dollar threshold that triggers the QBS process?

No. Unlike formal and informal purchase and construction and repair contracts, there are no cost thresholds that trigger the requirements of the Mini-Brooks Act. Unless the local government exempts itself from these requirements under G.S. 143-64.32, the requirements of G.S. 143-64.31 apply regardless of whether the estimated cost of the contract is $100 or $1 million.

7.6. Can price be solicited and considered in reviewing proposals from interested firms?

No. The Mini-Brooks Act specifically requires the local government to initially consider proposals based on demonstrated competency and qualifications "without regard to fee other than unit price . . . and no costs or fees, other than unit price information, may be solicited, submitted, or considered as part of the selection process."[2] Consequently, local governments may not solicit proposed fees in its RFQ, firms may not provide this information in their responses to the RFQ, and cost or fees may not be discussed or considered until the local government has completed its evaluation process, ranked the firms, and identified the best qualified.

7.7. What is "unit price," and can it be solicited?

The Mini-Brooks Act allows solicitation and consideration of unit price in the RFQ process. While the statute does not define "unit price," this term is commonly understood to mean pricing in standard units, such as hourly rates. While the local government is permitted to solicit unit price information, and firms are permitted to provide this information, the solicitation process cannot be structured in a way that could readily lead to an estimation of total fees for the project. For example, a local government could not solicit hourly rates and also ask for estimates of the total number of hours needed to complete the project because this could lead to a calculation of a total estimated fee (hourly rate × number of hours = total fee).

7.8. Other than price, are there any other limitations on information that can be solicited?

Yes. G.S. 143-64.31(f) prohibits a local government from soliciting or considering work product or design during the selection process. In addition, firms are prohibited from submitting work product or design to the local government. However, the statute does allow examples of prior completed work to be solicited, submitted, and considered when determining demonstrated competence and qualifications, and the statute encourages discussion of concepts or approaches to the project, including impact on project schedules.

---

2. G.S. 143-64.31(a), & (f).

7.9. When can price be considered?

After evaluating RFQ responses submitted by interested firms, a local government can negotiate a "fair and reasonable" price for the contract with the firm it has determined is the best qualified based on the evaluation criteria used to evaluate responses. The local government can also consider price if it exempts itself from the requirements of the Mini-Brooks Act under G.S. 143-64.32, which is discussed in section III, below.

7.10. What if negotiations with the best qualified firm fail?

If the local government is not able to negotiate a fair and reasonable contract price with the best qualified firm, it must terminate negotiations with that firm and initiate negotiations with the next best qualified firm. This requirement suggests that firms should be ranked in order of their qualifications and competence when responses to the RFQ are evaluated.

7.11. What if negotiations with the next best qualified firm fail?

While G.S. 143-64.31 does not specifically authorize continued negotiations with firms beyond the next best qualified, it is reasonable to interpret the statute to allow this. Under the federal Brooks Act, continued negotiations with lower ranked firms in priority order is actually required, obligating the agency head to undertake negotiations with the next qualified firm on the list and "continuing the process until an agreement is reached."[3] Given that North Carolina's Mini-Brooks Act is patterned after federal law, it is reasonable to assume that the intent of G.S. 143-64.31 is to give similar authorization to continue negotiations with subsequent firms until a contract agreement is eventually reached, assuming the local government wishes to do so. In the alternative, a local government could stop all negotiations and start over in the hope of a more successful outcome, or it could exempt itself from the QBS process requirements entirely under G.S. 143-64.32, which is discussed in section III, below.

7.12. Must the RFQ be formally advertised?

No. The Mini-Brooks Act does not require formal advertisement like formal purchase and construction contracts under G.S. 143-129(b). Instead, the local government must "announce all requirements" for the services sought, though the statute does not define what "announce" means. When a word is not specifically defined, it is given its plain meaning for purposes of statutory interpretation. Webster's defines "announce" as "to make publically known; to proclaim."[4] So, the announcement must be done in some public fashion and for some reasonable period of time to allow firms the opportunity to respond. Local governments employ various announcement strategies, such as posting on the local government's website, advertising in trade journals or the newspaper, or contacting firms directly. Regardless of which method is used, the goal is to get competition for the services needed to secure the best qualified firm.

7.13. Do minority business participation requirements apply?

Yes. The local government must make a good faith effort to notify minority firms of the opportunity to submit their qualifications for the services sought. The statute does not specify what these good faith efforts must consist of, so a good practice is to use the same methods as those used to encourage minority participation in informal construction and repair contracts. (See Chapter 4 for a full discussion of informal HUB requirements.) This is another reason to think broadly about the methods to use in announcing the requirements for the services sought.

7.14. Must a minimum number of responses be received?

No. Unlike formal construction contracts, which require a minimum of three bids in order to open bids and award a contract, the Mini-Brooks Act does not require the local government to receive a minimum number of responses before any can be considered, so presumably if only one response is received, the local government may still consider the qualifications of that firm, negotiate price, and award a contract.

---

3. 40 U.S.C. § 1104(b).
4. Merriam-Webster's Collegiate Dictionary (10th ed. 2002).

7.15. Must responses be submitted sealed?

No. The Mini-Brooks Act does not require responses to be sealed, but the local government can elect to require this if it chooses. If it chooses to do so, the local government should include this requirement in the RFQ.

7.16. Must responses be opened at a public opening?

No. The Mini-Brooks Act does not require a public bid opening, and local governments normally do not elect to set a specific time and location for opening responses. If a deadline is set for receiving responses, this deadline should be included in the RFQ.

7.17. Are responses a matter of public record?

Yes. Unless the local government requires responses to be submitted sealed, responses will be open to public inspection when received by the local government. If responses are required to be submitted sealed, they will be open to public inspection after they are unsealed (literally, when the envelopes are opened). In addition, the RFQ, rankings, and any other written evaluations of qualifications and responses also will be open to the public and subject to inspection by anyone, including the firms that have submitted responses.

7.18. Can firms be interviewed as part of the evaluation process?

Yes. Although the Mini-Brooks Act does not specifically authorize interviews with respondents, the statute does not prohibit this either. Because the focus of the QBS process is on the qualifications and competence of the firms competing for the contract, it is reasonable to interpret the statute to allow local governments to conduct interviews with firms during the evaluation process in order to fully assess each firm's qualifications for the project. However, the local government must refrain from discussing or negotiating a contract price until it has completed its evaluations, ranked all firms, and identified the firm it considers to be the best qualified.

7.19. What is the standard of award?

Under the Mini-Brooks Act, the local government may award the contract to the "best qualified" firm on the "basis of demonstrated competence and qualification for the type of professional services required." This standard of award differs significantly from the lowest responsive, responsible bidder standard of award that applies to competitively bid contracts in that it focuses on the qualifications of the firm and not on cost.

This standard of award affords the local government a great deal of discretion in determining which firm to award the contract. Many local governments use point systems for scoring the qualifications of responding firms, and this system may prove helpful in guiding the evaluation process. However, the local government may legitimately take into account subjective factors, such as style, communications skills, and conceptual approaches to a project.

7.20. Is governing board approval required for contract award?

No. The Mini-Brooks Act does not require that the governing board award the contract. However, a local government may require governing board approval under its own local policies.

7.21. What are "resident firm" preferences, and do they apply?

G.S. 143-64.31(a1) requires reciprocal state resident firm preferences. This means that the local government must give preference to "resident" firms in this state over "nonresident" firms from another state to the same extent that the other state grants a resident preference to its in-state firms. A "resident" firm is one that has paid unemployment taxes or income taxes in North Carolina and whose principal place of business is located in this state. Note that this is not a "local preference" in the sense that a firm in one geographic area of this state, such as a city or county, can be given preference over a firm from another in-state geographic area. Since this type of preference requires an analysis of price, it likely would apply only if the local government exempted itself from the Mini-Brooks Act.

III. Mini-Brooks Act Exemption

In some instances a local government may choose to exempt itself from the requirements of the Mini-Brooks Act. For an exemption to be legally valid, and the resulting contract itself to be legally valid, the exemption requirements must be strictly followed.

7.22. How does a local government exempt itself from the Mini-Brooks Act?

G.S. 143-64.32 authorizes a local government to exempt itself from the Mini-Brooks Act, which means it will not be required to use the QBS process and may select an architect, engineer, or surveyor through whatever method it chooses or award a contract without utilizing any process at all. The statute does not impose much in the way of requirements for utilizing the exemption—it simply requires that a local government put the exemption in writing. However, the exemption is capped at $50,000, meaning that the estimated cost of the contract cannot exceed this amount. Contracts with an estimated cost of $50,000 or more cannot be exempted, and the QBS process must be used.

7.23. Must the governing board approve an exemption?

Governing board approval is not required, but many local governments choose to do so anyway. If the local government chooses not to require governing board approval, the written exemption can be executed by any official or employee authorized to make this decision.

7.24. Is there a particular form required for the exemption?

The statute does not require the exemption to be in any particular form, only that the exemption be put in writing. See Appendix 7A for a sample board resolution and a memo to the file.

7.25. What justification must be given for the exemption?

G.S. 143-64.32 does not require the local government to provide any justification for utilizing the exemption. The statute merely requires that the exemption be in writing and the estimated cost of the contract be less than $50,000. Although local governments are not required to provide a justification for using the exemption, they may choose to do so as long as the justification is not for an illegal purpose (for example, citing a justification that constitutes unlawful discrimination).

7.26. Can price be solicited if the exemption is used?

Yes. If the local government exercises the exemption, the contract is exempt from all requirements and restrictions of the Mini-Brooks Act, including the prohibition against soliciting price. This is one of the more common reasons why local governments choose to exercise the exemption. By doing so, the local government can conduct an RFQ process that specifically solicits the total estimated fees for the service.

7.27. Can the exemption be used for construction management at-risk, design-build, design-build bridging, and public-private partnership contracts?

Legally, yes. From a practical standpoint, however, since the exemption is capped at $50,000, it is highly unlikely that it would be available for use on an alternative construction delivery method contract, as those contracts typically are well in excess of this amount.

7.28. Can a local government adopt a "blanket" exemption?

Local governments often prefer to have exemptions approved by their governing boards but may find it cumbersome to take each individual exemption to the board for adoption, especially when the contracts involve small projects. And sometimes a local government may want to put an architect or engineer on retainer for a period of time, such as a fiscal year, to call upon on a case-by-case basis but may not have any specific projects in mind when the architect or engineer is hired. Sometimes referred to as "blanket" exemptions, these arrangements are not authorized under the Mini-Brooks Act.

G.S. 143-64.32 states that a local government may exempt "particular projects" from the requirements of the Mini-Brooks Act. Although multiple projects could be included in one exemption, the language of the statute suggests that "blanket exemptions" are not authorized. While the courts have not yet decided this question, the N.C. Board of Examiners for Engineers and Surveyors has taken the position that exemptions must be granted on a project-by-project basis, so an engineer runs the risk of violating licensing requirements by responding to a RFQ that solicits price if the exemption of that project is not legally valid. To avoid an inadvertent violation of the statute (by any party), the safer course is to assume that blanket exemptions are not authorized and that the exemption must be adopted on a project-by-project basis. However, it does not seem inconsistent with the statute to include multiple specific projects in one resolution or exemption document if the local government has identified several specific projects for which it plans to award contracts. Furthermore, given that governing board approval is not statutorily required, the board could authorize an employee, such as the manager, to grant exemptions.

7.29. Can the exemption be used on federally funded projects?

If the project involves federal funding, the state exemption under G.S. 143-64.32 will likely violate federal procurement requirements, as there is no parallel or comparable exemption under federal law. A local government wishing to consider utilizing the Mini-Brooks Act exemption on a federally funded project should consult the federal agency providing the funds.

Appendix 7A Sample Mini-Brooks Act Exemption

Option 1: Governing Board Resolution

RESOLUTION EXEMPTING [*NAME OF PROJECT(S)*]
FROM G.S. 143-64.31

WHEREAS, G.S. 143-64.31 requires the initial solicitation and evaluation of firms to perform architectural, engineering, or surveying services (collectively "design services") to be based on qualifications and without regard to fee;

WHEREAS, the [*name of local government*] proposes to enter into one or more contracts for design services for work on [*name or description of the project(s) being exempted by the resolution*]; and

WHEREAS, G.S. 143-64.32 authorizes units of local government to exempt contracts for design services from the qualifications-based selection requirements of G.S. 143-64.32 if the estimated fee is less than $50,000; and

WHEREAS, the estimated fee for design services for the above-described project is less than $50,000.

NOW, THEREFORE, THE [*Governing Board*] OF THE [*Unit of Government*] RESOLVES:

Section 1. The above-described project(s) is hereby made exempt from the provisions of G.S. 143-64.31.

Section 2. This resolution shall be effective upon adoption.

[*add appropriate signature lines and seal*]

Notes:

1. The exemption is *only* authorized for contracts with an estimated fee of less than $50,000.
2. No justification for exercising the exemption is required; the local government may include a justification if it wishes to do so by adding an additional WHEREAS clause stating the justification.

Option 2: Memo to the File

[*Date*]

-MEMORANDUM-

TO: Project File for [*name of project; including project number if applicable*]

FROM: [*name of employee*]

RE: Exemption from G.S. 143-64.31

The contract for architectural, engineering, or surveying services for the above-referenced project is hereby exempted from the requirements of G.S. 143-64.31. The estimated total cost of this contract is less than $50,000.

Signature: ______________________________

[*name of employee*]

Notes:

1. The exemption is *only* authorized for contracts with an estimated fee of less than $50,000.
2. No justification for exercising the exemption is required; the local government may include a justification if it wishes to do so by adding an additional sentence stating the justification.
3. The exemption should be retained in the project file.

Printed in the USA
CPSIA information can be obtained
at www.ICGtesting.com
CBHW071332210224
4568CB00006B/74

9 781560 117605